The CILIP Guidelines for Secondary School Libraries

THIRD EDITION

Edited by
Sue Shaper

for the School Libraries Group of CILIP

Working Group

Sue Bastone, Elizabeth Bentley, June Brooks, Sheila Compton,
Annie Everall, Rebecca Hemming, John Iona, Rebecca Jones,
Sally McIntosh, Sarah Masters, Michael Margerison, Caroline Roche,
Sue Shaper, Susan Staniforth, Adrian Thompson, Karen Usher

facet publishing

© CILIP: the Chartered Institute of Library and Information
   Professionals 2014

Published by Facet Publishing,
7 Ridgmount Street, London WC1E 7AE
www.facetpublishing.co.uk

Facet Publishing is wholly owned by CILIP: the Chartered Institute of
Library and Information Professionals.

British Library Cataloguing in Publication Data
A catalogue record for this book is available from the British Library.

ISBN 978-1-85604-969-6

First published by The Library Association 1998
Second edition 2004
This third edition 2014

Text printed on FSC accredited material.

Typeset from editors' files by Flagholme Publishing Services in 10/14 pt
Palatino Linotype and Humanist 521.
Printed and made in Great Britain by CPI Group (UK) Ltd, Croydon,
CR0 4YY.

Contents

Foreword

A love of reading unlocks many doors and the school library is so often where this starts. Head teachers recognize the contribution that a good school library makes to a thriving school. They know that pupils who read for pleasure usually achieve more; they also know that a well stocked and well run school library improves teaching and learning.

We need to get the best out of our school librarians. They are highly qualified members of staff and can be used as a resource by teachers and pupils to make the most of information sources, to develop reading and research skills and to support the curriculum with the right materials.

Librarians bring a unique knowledge and skill set into the school, complementing the work of teachers whilst instilling a love of reading for pleasure among pupils from a different perspective and through different kinds of activities.

In many schools, the library is at the heart of its ethos and is a welcoming environment for pupils with a whole range of needs, supporting education in its widest sense.

I welcome these guidelines, which value the role of the school library and celebrate the skill and dedication of librarians.

Russell Hobby
General Secretary
National Association of Head Teachers

Key recommendations

CILIP recommends that:

1   The school recognizes the school library and the librarian as essential in supporting teaching and learning.
2   The school recognizes the essential leadership role of the librarian and seeks to appoint a full-time Chartered Librarian with administrative support.
3   The librarian participates in the school's improvement planning process with the same rigour as other academic staff.
4   The environment of the school library supports its role as a whole-school learning resource.
5   The school supports the vital role that sufficient quality resources play in stimulating learning and maximizes the impact of this investment by managing resources centrally.
6   The librarian takes a lead role in the development of students' information literacy skills to enable all students to become independent, lifelong learners.
7   The librarian plays a lead role in developing a whole-school reading culture, promoting literacy and reading for pleasure.
8   The librarian is proactive in marketing and promoting services, resources and library use.
9   The librarian regularly evaluates the performance of the library.
10 The librarian works with key internal and external partners to improve the service provision of the school library.

Introduction

These *Guidelines* are the recommendations of CILIP: the Chartered Institute of Library and Information Professionals for the effective management of secondary school libraries. They are addressed to head teachers, governors and all who are involved in the strategic management of education and who want to understand the potential of a good school library and how they can realize it. They are also intended to provide those who manage school libraries with practical guidance and material for advocacy. Whilst many of the resources that are mentioned have a UK focus, we believe that the underlying principles are applicable for an international audience.

It has been a privilege to build upon the work of the experienced practitioners who wrote the two earlier editions of these guidelines. The Library Association's *Guidelines for Secondary School Libraries* (Tilke, 1998) and *The CILIP Guidelines for Secondary School Libraries* (Barrett and Douglas, 2004) have been highly influential in guiding the development of secondary school libraries. This new edition addresses recent developments in educational thinking and information technology, in keeping with our vision of school librarians as forward thinkers in a changing world.

These guidelines are, by their very nature, aspirational and in an ideal world all schools would adhere to the principles outlined. However, the practical difficulties, not least of finding the right budget and personnel, mean that some schools will take the approach of 'a work in progress'. Career paths vary considerably but professionalism drives a common ongoing search for improvement. The advice offered here should help schools to prioritize and implement improvements to library provision over time.

At the heart of these *Guidelines* are ten recommendations (see page vii) that are the foundations of excellent school library provision. CILIP hopes that these recommendations will be accepted and put into practice in every secondary school. Being aware that its vision for school library provision depends on partnerships with a wide range of stakeholders, CILIP also commends these *Guidelines* to the attention of education managers, policy makers and government.

The new edition has been revised by the current national committee of CILIP's School Libraries Group, comprising:

Sue Bastone MCLIP, Head of Learning Resources, LVS Ascot

Elizabeth Bentley DipLib DipEd BA(Hons) MCLIP, Librarian, Addey and Stanhope School, South London

June Brooks BA MCLIP, formerly Lead Adviser with Hampshire School Library Service

Sheila Compton BA(Hons) MCLIP, Librarian, Dame Alice Owen School, Hertfordshire

Annie Everall OBE BA(Hons)Lib MCLIP, Director, Authors Aloud UK

Rebecca Hemming BA MusB(Hons) MSc PGCE DipArtsMan, Head of Library, University College School, North London

John Iona MA BA(Hons), Librarian, Oasis Academy, Enfield

Rebecca Jones PhD BA(Hons) MCLIP, Learning Enrichment and Support Co-ordinator and Librarian, Malvern St James, Worcestershire

Sally McIntosh BA MSc MCLIP, Learning Resources Manager, Heanor Gate Science College, Derbyshire

Michael Margerison BA(Hons) PgDipILM, Librarian and Learning Resources Centre Manager, The Elmgreen School, South London

Sarah Masters BSc MCLIP, Multi-media Research Manager, Thomas Deacon Academy, Peterborough

Caroline Roche MA MCLIP, Librarian, Eltham College, South London

Sue Shaper DipLib MA(Ed) FCLIP HonFCLIP, Library Resources Director, The Broxbourne School, Hertfordshire

Susan Staniforth BA(Hons) MCLIP, Manager, Library Services for Education, Gloucestershire

Adrian Thompson BA(Ed)Hons, Learning Resource Centre Manager,

Laisterdyke Business and Enterprise College, Bradford, West Yorkshire

Karen Usher MCLIP HonFCLIP, Librarian, South Hunsley School and Sixth Form College, East Riding of Yorkshire

Notes

1 Many school libraries are now known as learning resource centres, LRCs or open learning centres. Similarly, the school librarian may be called the learning resource centre manager. In these *Guidelines* the terms 'school library' and 'school librarian' are used to refer to all of the above.

2 The developments and improvements identified within schools and school departments may be known as development plans or improvement plans. In these *Guidelines* the term 'improvement plan' is used to refer to either of these or any other document produced by the school identifying areas and targets for development and improvement.

3 Some areas have a support and resource service for schools that may be known as a schools' library service, education library service or schools' resource service. Within these *Guidelines* the term 'school library service' or 'SLS' is used to refer to all such services.

4 A complete list of references follows Chapter 10. Many of these are excellent sources for further reading but in order to avoid the guidelines becoming unwieldy, a smaller number of selected texts and websites are recommended at appropriate points throughout the book rather than in a bibliography at the end. The intention has not been to provide a comprehensive literature review because it was felt that to guide the reader to a few key sources would be more helpful.

Notes

Abbreviations

AASL	American Association of School Librarians
ACLIP	Associate Member of the Chartered Institute of Library and Information Professionals
AIDA	A marketing mnemonic standing for *Awareness, Interest, Desire, Action*
ASLA	Australian School Library Association
CILIP	The Chartered Institute of Library and Information Professionals
CPD	Continuing professional development
DfE	Department for Education
DfES	Department for Education and Skills *now DfE*
FCLIP	Fellow of the Chartered Institute of Library and Information Professionals
IASL	International Association of School Librarianship
ICT	Information and communication technology
IFLA	International Federation of Library Associations and Institutions
IL	Information literacy
ILG	Information Literacy Group (part of CILIP)
INSET	In-service education and training
ISI	Independent Schools Inspectorate (www.isi.net)
KPI	Key performance indicators
LILAC	Annual information literacy conference run by the ILG
MCLIP	Chartered Member of the Chartered Institute of Library and Information Professionals
MLE	Managed learning environment

OFQUAL	Office of Qualifications and Examinations Regulation
Ofsted	Office for Standards in Education, Children's Services and Skills (www.ofsted.gov.uk)
PTA	Parent–teacher association
SEF	Self-evaluation form
SID	Safer Internet Day
SLA	School Library Association
SLG	School Libraries Group (part of CILIP)
SLS	School library service
UNESCO	United Nations Educational, Scientific and Cultural Organization
VLE	Virtual learning environment
WAN	Wide area network

The school librarian and learning: CILIP's vision

CILIP recommends that the school recognizes the school library and the librarian as essential in supporting teaching and learning. This means that:

- the school library is an independent, academic department
- the school librarian is head of that department
- the school library is a whole-school resource
- the school library is an inclusive service.

Introduction

Since the last edition of these guidelines (Barrett and Douglas, 2004) there have been unprecedented changes in all sorts of technologies which, in turn, have altered the way we think about education, particularly in the debate surrounding how our young people should learn and what learning looks like in the 21st century. At the moment, we are preparing them for jobs that may not yet exist and for a world that has never before been so connected; one that will become even more connected in ways that we cannot even dream of as yet. This has led to some questioning of the value of having a school librarian and library, when everything is freely available on the internet without apparently requiring the mediation of a librarian. However, as the discourse on pedagogy changes and widens to include evidence-based learning, independent and collaborative learning and guided inquiry, libraries will become a 'learning commons' (Loerstscher et al., 2011) where librarians are no longer just the keepers of books or even gatekeepers in the traditional sense; they will become the people who prepare students for the future we cannot yet see, using tools that have not yet been invented. The service provided will not be restricted to the school day, with a rigid timetable, fixed furniture, selected resources and set patterns of use. Library services will be available all the time and choice of resources, use of space and services will all be flexible and determined by the users' needs. Now and in the future, the school librarian helps every learner to begin a relationship with the library that should be a lifelong relationship: what happens at school prepares them for what happens at college or university or at work or at the public library.

The changes in technology present challenges but, as the new tools are invented, they are being assimilated into the work of the librarian. We are currently witnessing the development of the e-book and the complexities of providing access to both print and electronic resources. This means that the nomenclature currently differentiates between the library and the e-library or digital library but over time, as the technology beds down, this will revert to being inclusive. Previous technological innovations, such as audio books or videos have been assimilated. Soon electronic and print resources and social media will be reconciled into what we will still call a library (Lankes, 2011). Even the Texas library that has no physical books is still called a library (Hicks, 2013). What is important is what the librarian does in the space that is called the library. The focus should be on the outcomes and impact of the service provided, whereas the collection and artefacts within are merely the tools that are used.

A school librarian's business is education and learning, through the medium of a library. It is about teaching lifelong competencies: whether that is finding effectively the information needed or being able to critically evaluate what has been found and then being able to use that information in a completely new way. It is about developing readers who love reading and continually working towards a culture of reading for pleasure within the school in a way that is very different to the experience of exploring a set text in a classroom. It is about developing a community of learners who see the library as their space; a place in which they can pursue their interests whether they are related to the curriculum or not.

None of this can be achieved by one person alone and so the school librarian has to be able to see their work within the context of the school improvement plan (or whatever document drives the development of their school) and to align their efforts strategically with the school's objectives and work effectively with a wide range of colleagues. It needs a highly developed level of interpersonal skills with the courage and stamina to be a leader. This in turn requires a high level of competence and knowledge of educational pedagogy (in addition to all the skills and knowledge of librarianship) in order to have credibility with colleagues and students. This is why CILIP recommends that schools should appoint Chartered Librarians (see Chapter 2).

Why schools should have librarians and libraries

The aim of all schools is to produce well educated young people who are ready to take their place in society; who have the knowledge, skills and resilience for life in the 21st century; and who are equipped with the hard currency of the best grades they can achieve in order that they can move on successfully to their chosen path. The government measures a school's success through its tests and examination results and this is where the research evidence in support of school librarians and libraries is unequivocal. Successive University of Colorado studies have revealed that students attain better grades in schools that have a school librarian and school library. There was also a clear correlation between how well resourced the school library was (i.e. whether the school chose to employ a well qualified librarian and provide him/her with a good budget) and the level of attainment of its students. This correlation was confirmed in relation to reading attainment in a study that looked at data between 2005 and 2011 in the 50 US states (Lance and Hofschire, 2012). An infographic (Library Research Service, 2013) gives further information about these Colorado impact studies.

Whilst employers complain about school leavers not having the literacy, creativity and skills they need (e.g. CBI, 2013), the British Lifelong Study (Taylor, 2011) showed that the more students read, the more likely they were to end up in a professional or managerial job by the age of 33. Sullivan and Brown's longitudinal study found that 'children who read for pleasure are likely to do significantly better at school than their peers' (Institute of Education, 2013). Frequent reading helps students to get better at processing text and thinking critically and creatively – skills which are increasingly important for the new knowledge economy (Robinson, 2011). Librarians can play a vital part in addressing these issues.

How school librarians support teaching

All teachers need a school librarian to:

1 **Provide the right kind of resources for their lessons and students.** This means ensuring there are sufficient and appropriate materials to support a lesson or sequence of lessons. It may mean working collaboratively by planning lessons together and team teaching, with clarity and professional respect between the different roles. The librarian can enrich the lessons for the teacher as well as the students by being knowledgeable about the range of resources available for their particular topic which, in turn, helps the teachers to remain current and refresh their teaching. The librarian will also have a unique overview of requirements across the school, providing materials that are not subject- or lesson-specific.
2 **Encourage and develop them as reading champions so that they can model reading for pleasure to their students.** The adults in a young person's life are influential role models and if teachers share their own reading with their students then that will send a powerful message about the importance of reading and how it relates to success.
3 **Lead or shape the development of the information literacy strategy across the school.** School librarians need to take every opportunity to demonstrate to colleagues how they can help transform learning within their school. Leading the occasional INSET session with staff raises librarians' profile; shows strong support for them by the senior leaders in the school; and sends an unequivocal message that they can be a part of the solution to the specific challenges being addressed in a school. Information literacy cannot be delivered by school librarians on their own – it must be shared across all staff.
4 **Provide them with the right kind of resources for their own learning and professional development.** Librarians keep abreast of the latest educational developments and disseminate these to teaching colleagues.

How school librarians support learning

The publication *School Libraries: a right* (CILIP, 2011) declares that all students need someone to:

- support and encourage their development as confident readers who enjoy reading widely and regularly for pleasure
- support their curriculum-based needs
- develop them as competent and critical users of the huge amount of information available, so that they become lifelong learners
- provide a safe and secure learning environment
- support their individual emotional, cultural and leisure needs.

Of course, there are other people in schools who make vital contributions to these areas but CILIP believes that no one else provides such a comprehensive and accessible service so cost-effectively. The librarian is uniquely placed within a school community to mediate and facilitate learning to individuals, classes, year groups and the whole school. Librarians work with students:

1 **To encourage and develop them as readers.** A core strand of school librarianship will always be about developing readers, as this is the primary literacy. This is not to say that the librarian has sole responsibility for this in a school but the librarian is key to the fostering of reading for pleasure and approaches this very differently to teaching colleagues.
2 **To support their learning in the classroom.** This can range from working alongside teachers in the classroom to one-to-one support in helping with homework after the lesson.
3 **To provide opportunities for enrichment and intellectual stimulation beyond the curriculum.** Librarians are the original 'enrichment co-ordinators' within their school. The library is the place where what is not learned in the classroom can be experienced. Teachers teach the curriculum and rarely have the time to go beyond that in the classroom but there is more to knowledge building than just that which appears in the examination syllabus or national curriculum; the library provides a neutral space in which a student may pursue their own interests, building social and cultural capital.
4 **To provide intellectual and emotional support.** The pastoral role of the school librarian and the neutral space of the library is not always the first aspect thought of as being part of the librarian's work but research shows that it can be crucial to young people's learning (Shaper and Streatfield,

2012). It is well established that good learning happens only when there are good relationships between students and teachers and the school librarian needs to be able to cultivate an equally strong bond of trust with individual members of the learning community. Aside from the challenge of learning, the librarian may be the person to whom a student turns to at a time of personal need. Furthermore, the librarian's knowledge of contemporary literature for young adults means they are ideally placed to provide reading materials that, for example, build self-esteem or share problems.

Further information

Markless, S. (ed.), Bentley, E., Pavey, S., Shaper, S., Todd, S. and Webb, C. (2009) *The Innovative School Librarian: thinking outside the box,* Facet Publishing.
School Libraries Group (2007) *Designed for Learning* video, www.cilip.org.uk/cilip/advocacy-awards-and-projects/advocacy-and-campaigns/school-libraries/briefings-and-resources-1.

2

Staffing and management

CILIP recommends that the school recognizes the essential leadership role of the librarian and seeks to appoint a full-time chartered librarian with administrative support. This means that:

- the librarian has professional library qualifications and is committed to ongoing professional development
- the librarian is fully integrated into the academic staff of the school and is given the same status, voice, support and training as other departmental heads
- the librarian has sufficient administrative support to allow time to fulfil the leadership, management and teaching requirements of the role.

Introduction

The management of the school library will determine the impact the library has on achievement. Research has shown that where the school's senior management actively supports and endorses the librarian's leadership of the school library the librarian is more effective in supporting key educational objectives (Streatfield, Shaper and Rae-Scott, 2010; Streatfield and Rae-Scott, 2013). Williams, Wavell and Coles (2001) have also demonstrated that where a skilled librarian is empowered by management to collaborate effectively with teaching departments the impact on learning is optimized. However, a major factor in maximizing the impact of the library on the whole school is the individual school librarian. The learning librarian is a reflective practitioner: one who keeps up to date, seeks opportunities for professional development, is a member of professional organizations, understands teaching and learning and its development and knows the curriculum.

Assuming that a learning librarian is in post, this chapter outlines the management responsibilities of the school librarian and defines how the role fits into the broader educational structure.

The school librarian within the school management structure

The management of the library must reflect and support school policies. To achieve this, librarians must be integrated into the school's management structure at a high enough level to have impact. Recognizing their professional knowledge and skills (CILIP, 2013c) they must be empowered to make decisions. The recent Ofsted (2013b) report on improving literacy states: 'Where librarians are fully integrated into the management structure of the school, they have an opportunity to influence debate and to enhance the library's contribution to pupils' progress.'

To enable this to happen, CILIP recommends that the librarian:

- is line managed by a senior leadership team member with responsibility for curriculum development
- is consulted and included in improvement planning to influence the strategic direction of the school
- has direct access to the strategic management of the school, so that the library can play a full role in school improvement
- has head of department status so that the librarian can listen to, understand and meet the needs of all departments within the school and play a full and proactive part in improvement planning on a par with other heads of departments
- is responsible for feeding into the annual reporting process in line with academic departments
- is not associated with any one particular teaching department and works effectively across the curriculum
- has a relationship with the governing body in line with other heads of department
- is included in all staff appraisals and training and participates in the delivery of relevant staff INSET
- is salaried at a level commensurate with other departmental heads.

Human resources and continuous professional development (CPD)

Staffing arrangements in secondary school libraries differ widely throughout the UK (Streatfield, Shaper and Rae-Scott, 2010). CILIP recommends that a full-time Chartered Librarian manages the library, supported by library assistant(s). Where libraries are provided on more than one site in a school, it is important that both sites are staffed full time with sufficient time to have scheduled meetings. A case study of staffing organization and progression is provided in Appendix 5.

Where librarians do have to work alone, it is important that they are able to manage their time effectively and professionally, enabling quality time to be spent working with students and teaching colleagues whilst ensuring adequate breaks in line with current health and safety requirements. This means they have to decide about the importance of different tasks and prioritize. Investigating the amount of time needed for housekeeping tasks and showing the number of staff-hours required to carry out all functions of the library effectively can provide a persuasive basis for a request for library assistants or administrative support.

Performance management

School librarians should be part of the school's performance management scheme, with:

- an annual review of performance with target setting. Targets may include:
  - increase the number of library visits from an identified group of students
  - deliver or develop a new service, e.g. foreign-language films
  - develop an e-books project to support Sixth Form research within an identified department
  - attend three professional network meetings and identify developments and best practice that can be used to improve the library
- an annual review of the post's job description and grading
- targets, at least one of which should focus on student learning and/or attainment and one on professional development
- regular discussions with the line manager
- access to relevant external training and development opportunities
- adequate cover arrangements in place for periods of sickness or absence for training days.

Continuous professional development

Rapid development in librarianship, information management, ICT and the education sector means that it is essential that the school librarian actively engages in CPD. This encompasses a wide variety of activity from temporary placements, participation in training and professional reading to active networking, involvement with professional organizations and working towards higher educational qualifications. Librarians should also participate in whole-school INSET and be prepared to deliver induction and INSET training to colleagues.

Librarians should manage their own CPD in collaboration with the school's staff development officer. It is useful to maintain a professional development portfolio and to use it as the basis for the annual appraisal. The librarian must have access to external training opportunities and be able to attend appropriate meetings and exhibitions. It is vital that the librarian has time to network with other school librarians. In order to develop professionally, school librarians need to participate actively in professional groups and networks in a setting wider than the school, where they will frequently be the only information professional. CILIP, CILIP's SLG, SLA and membership of local school library services provide excellent opportunities for professional participation. Web-based communities and e-lists are also invaluable sources of professional discussion.

Useful links for CPD

American Association of School Librarians, www.ala.org/aasl.

Australian School Library Association, www.asla.org.au.

Chartered Institute of Library and Information Professionals,
  www.cilip.org.uk.

Heart of the School website, heartoftheschool.edublogs.org.

International Association of School Librarianship: School Libraries Online,
  www.iasl-online.org.

School Libraries Group, www.cilip.org.uk/about/special-interest-groups/
  schoollibrariesgroup.

School Library Association, www.sla.org.uk.

Discussion lists

LIS-EDUC: Library Services for Education. To join LIS-EDUC, send an
e-mail message to jiscmail@jiscmail.ac.uk with the command: join lis-educ
firstname lastname.

School Librarians' Network. To subscribe, send an e-mail with 'Subscribe' in
the subject to sln-subscribe@yahoogroups.com.

Responsibilities

The librarian has discrete responsibilities under the following headings, the
first four of which are covered in this chapter and the remainder in other parts
of these guidelines as indicated:

- financial planning and budget management
- interviewing and appraising staff
- behaviour management
- management of ICT
- improvement planning (see Chapter 3)
- library environment (see Chapter 4)
- resources management (see Chapter 5)
- marketing, promotion and advocacy (see Chapter 8)
- evaluation (see Chapter 9)
- partnership management (see Chapter 10).

Financial planning and budget management

Financial planning and budget management are the two processes that
govern all library funding. An example of a budget for setting up a new
library is shown in Appendix 6, together with an exemplar of an annual
budget for an established library.

Sound financial planning must precede budget management. To be seen as
authoritative this will pay due regard to:

- national and local standards and guidelines
- current educational initiatives
- the library's improvement plan, which is part of the whole-school
improvement plan

- current costs
- expectations of future demand
- realistic estimations of the cost of capital projects and future developments.

Standards and guidelines

Standards and guidelines are useful tools in identifying the library's current position, which should be reviewed annually. Benchmarking or evaluation tools (e.g. Streatfield and Markless, 2004) may be used to inform judgements. The librarian will also be familiar with best practice across the education sector through professional reading, active partnership with the local school library service, where one is available, and involvement in professional organizations.

Educational initiatives

National and local initiatives that impact on the library's services and resources need to be part of the financial planning process. These may include curriculum changes, literacy programmes or ICT developments.

Improvement plan

The financial requirements of the library relate to whole-school targets and are detailed in the library's improvement plan. The plan should cover at least one year and may extend to 3–5 years to provide forward planning for future developments. Distinctions should be drawn between capital investment costs and ongoing increased maintenance costs. It is necessary to establish a school policy for funding software or electronic subscriptions that are accessible online or across the school network.

Current costs and expectations of future demand

Previous years' expenditure should be analysed and include elements for stock, periodicals, stationery, photocopying and maintenance/support contracts on equipment and software. This will help to build a picture of requirements and form the basis of a new budget request. Items that were required or requested but could not be provided due to a shortfall in a previous budget should be included in a separate section of the analysis. Future developments in the school and specific directions for the library need to be taken into account. Known costs or reasonable estimates should be indicated in order to provide senior management with the facts to support sound financial planning.

Capital projects and future developments

Capital projects are one-off expenses that are not part of the school's annual funding from which a budget is allocated. They might be for new furnishings, computer hardware and/or software (such as a library management system), or even for new resources needed to deliver a specific student learning outcome.

Requests for capital spending should, where possible, be related to outcomes that are measurable, such as reduced loss resulting from the installation of a security system. A bid should indicate the benefits to users as well as how the benefits will be measured. Where appropriate, it should include quotations for the proposed spend.

Future developments may include significant changes to the operation of the library such as a plan to change to e-book lending only for Sixth Form texts or a plan to significantly increase the amount of stock following the physical expansion of a library. Costs for future developments should be estimated as realistically as possible for both the implementation and development, including the ongoing impact on annual budget requirements over a number of years.

Budget management

Once a budget has been allocated, it must be well managed. It is useful to plan how funds will be spent over the whole year. Some institutions require this type of detailed planning, but even if they do not, it is sound management practice to be able to predict when money will be required from each budget section and to be able to account for funds already committed or spent. Whilst periodicals may require a monthly expenditure, it is wise to complete spending for most other resources before the end of the financial year, as unspent funds may be reclaimed rather than carried forward into the next financial year. Also, future budgets may be cut as a result of any underspend. It is recommended that school managers recognize that library spending needs to be spread across the year, and that an agreed level of underspend is allowed to be carried forward. This encourages considered purchasing and also enables newly published stock to be ordered at the beginning of the next financial year whilst the new budget is being finalized.

At any given time the librarian should have access to financial information and budget tracking data.

Staff management

Where library assistants are employed, it is important that they are well managed by the librarian. This means attention to:

- on-the-job training
- ongoing communication
- annual appraisal in line with other school support staff
- inclusion in whole staff INSET, when possible
- access to external training such as ACLIP certification (CILIP, 2013a).

All library staff need to be competent and confident computer users and skilled in using new technologies. They need CPD that focuses on:

- new technological developments
- issues and skills surrounding teaching and learning with electronic resources
- strategies for effective implementation of digital library services.

Student librarians play an important role in the running of some school libraries. They, too, need to be trained, given responsibility, and appraised. A useful toolkit for this purpose is available from the SLA, to their members only (School Library Association, 2008).

Behaviour management

Librarians are unlikely to receive training in behaviour management through their initial professional qualification, so it is important that training opportunities are made available to them. A great deal can be learned through observing teaching colleagues within the school.

Librarians must be aware of their duty of care and the whole-school policies regarding health and safety, safeguarding and first aid and to whom they are required to report these issues. In addition, in order to guarantee good behaviour and safeguarding, the library must have a staffing ratio commensurate with any other learning environment within the school. When considering staffing ratios the following factors should be considered:

- the children: their age, maturity, behaviour history
- the supervisor: someone new to the job or new to the school will need extra support
- the activity: library activities should be low risk
- the facilities: library facilities should be safe
- the location: the location of the library should be safe and close to help in case there is a problem.

Therefore, CILIP recommends that each school ensures that:

- the librarian has adult support in the library during regular busy periods
- all out-of-school-hours use by students is supervized
- proper emergency and evacuation procedures are in place
- the library is included in rotas for senior management duty cover
- the librarian is included in arrangements for disciplinary codes and procedures as well as the whole-school reward system
- the librarian has the status and authority to exercise behaviour management strategies in the school library, in line with school policies.

Management of ICT

ICT is now being integrated into all areas of teaching and learning and librarians should expect this to extend to the school library. ICT is a motivating tool which can engage students with learning and attitudinal and language difficulties, enriching the learning experience of all students. Librarians need to embrace ICT, participate in all that it offers to students and teachers and recognize how it inspires independent learning. All school librarians have a responsibility to foster the effective use of ICT through the selection of appropriate resources, and through the teaching of skills to enable effective student use of the new technologies.

Librarians can make an important contribution to the development of the school's digital services. Many have taken on the responsibility for intranet or website development for their school. This is a natural development for the school's information specialist, and can demonstrate and affirm the central role of the librarian as the school's knowledge manager. School librarians need to apprise themselves of the infrastructure and connectivity issues in their schools, and identify the areas where they can best contribute. Options may include:

- being part of any VLE development to ensure seamless access to the library's resources
- ensuring that the library catalogue is accessible over the intranet or any wider area network (WAN) developed by the school, such as a VLE or MLE
- arranging subscriptions to appropriate online services as an alternative to purchasing hard copy stock
- providing links to useful resource sites for teaching staff
- providing links from library internet computers or the library pages on the school intranet to bookmarked sites to support specific areas of work
- contributing to the school's daily news items on the website or intranet
- keeping up to date with web-based developments in the library management system that will enhance accessibility of resources where a VLE or an MLE is used
- providing website reviews for staff and students
- developing interactive pages on the school's intranet to promote reading and useful resources and library activities and services
- designing and managing the school's external website
- providing details and advice for the school on 'internet safety' and copyright issues.

3

Policies and planning

CILIP recommends that the librarian participates in the school's improvement planning process with the same rigour as other academic staff. This means that:

- the librarian has access to and works closely with all levels of leadership in order to plan library improvements in accordance with whole-school priorities
- planning and evaluation procedures are the same as other school departments, with high expectations of monitoring, consultation and reporting
- the library improvement plan is based on the agenda of the whole school, and is not just a reflection of the library policies.

Introduction

There are two main vehicles for articulating and achieving the vision for the school library. These are the library policy and the improvement plan. The librarian needs to state explicitly how the vision of the library's role, as explored in Chapter 1, will be realized. This may be expressed by developing the library's aims and objectives in a policy document or mission statement. The improvement plan document sets out how these aims and objectives will be achieved by setting targets, establishing time frames and costings and detailing measurable outcomes. Although the templates in Appendices 7, 8 and 9 may be used as a guide, the librarian should adopt the policy and improvement plan styles already in use by the school.

The school library policy

The school library policy should define how the library will help deliver the aims and objectives of the school and provide a vision for the library service. It reflects the ethos, aspirations and changing priorities of the whole school community. At the same time, it provides a practical framework for managing the school library and achieving its full potential. Alternatively a mission statement and a discrete series of supporting library policies can be used. These will indicate how the library supports teaching and learning, as well as including basic operational issues. As priorities and practices differ from school to school there is no one definitive list of policies that a secondary school should have and, rather than invest time developing a bank of policies all at once, it is recommended that only policies that are actually needed are created. Appendix 9 gives examples of different approaches to a policy about overdues.

Once created, the policy explains why the library does what it does. A policy by itself will never be truly effective. It needs to be implemented, embedded and regularly reviewed, to be successful. A procedure document (e.g. Appendix 9) shows how the policy is implemented.

Data should be collected for self-evaluation, or as KPI (Key Performance Indicators). These need to be reported to the line manager, senior leadership team, governors or board of directors as evidence of impact (Chapter 9 has more on self-evaluation).

General library policy guidelines

While each school library policy is a unique document, all policies will define the role of the school library in relation to:

- the curriculum and key education strategies
- learning and teaching methods within the school
- national standards and recommendations
- students' learning and developmental or pastoral needs
- teachers' learning and teaching needs
- raising achievement
- inspiring readers
- promoting information literacy.

Therefore a school library policy may generally include:

- aims and objectives of the school library
- the management structure and systems of the school library
- user and non-user involvement in the library's management
- resource management guidelines
- how the library contributes to information literacy skills development across the curriculum
- how the library promotes reading across the school
- how the library caters for individual learning needs to ensure equal access for all
- how the library works with internal and external partners (as in Chapter 10)
- how the school library is promoted
- how the school library is monitored and evaluated
- how and when the school library policy is to be revised.

Basic steps to develop a library policy

1 Assess the need for a new policy:
    - Is there already something in existence?
    - If yes, does it need rewriting/reviewing?
    - If no, then take steps to create a new document.
2 Research:
    - Network locally with other school librarians, maybe through sources suggested in Chapter 2.
    - Look at supportive websites such as SLG or the SLA.
    - Look for what has already been produced.
    - Look at how other libraries deal with the same issues.
3 Write the draft:
    - Use the school's own standard template for policies if there is one.
    - Focus the writing on the intended audience. Is the policy for library staff, students, governors, parents or teachers?
    - Policies should be in a positive written form.
4 Review the draft with stakeholders:
    - Get input from the stakeholders.
    - To gain credibility library policies need to link to other school policies.

For example a library policy on computer usage in the library needs to refer back to the whole school ICT policy and where there are any differences these will need to be clearly explained.

5 Obtain approval:
- Approval from appropriate management should be obtained in line with school procedures.

6 Publish the policy:
- Publish and distribute copies to the appropriate people.
- Make all policies available on the library homepages or where appropriate. Promote these through publications like the school prospectus, staff handbook, parental leaflets, displays, TV screens.

7 Continuing professional development:
- If training is needed on aspects of the policy (for library staff, students or teachers) then this should be delivered as appropriate.

8 Develop procedures:
- Develop any necessary procedures resulting from the policy.
- Review these procedures after a trial period. (Appendix 9 has an example of a flowchart for an overdues procedure).

9 Review:
- No policy is a static document.
- Revisit the policy annually to ensure that it reflects changes and developments in the library and responds to school-wide priorities.
- Plan for a structured revision every 2–3 years in line with whole-school practice.
- Involve the senior leadership team, the library committee or the governing body, as deemed appropriate, in any review.

The school library improvement plan or business plan

The improvement plan sets out to achieve the vision for the library and its services. It should demonstrate how the library will become more effective in supporting teaching and learning across the school. The improvement plan needs to adhere to the school's planning cycle. The library improvement plan should feed into the school's system, using templates and formats associated with the school-wide improvement plan. It should be written in line with other curriculum areas and involve stakeholders, especially other managers, as this may lead to mutually beneficial improvements and the library being included in other curriculum area plans.

The librarian should look at the priority areas for the school and ask how the library's services could support these main goals. The plan must be explicit about how the library will be delivering the main goals of the organization, such as raising literacy levels, or maximizing the learning opportunities offered by ICT. It should build on the findings of inspection or self-evaluation exercises. It is essential that the library improvement plan is based upon the agenda of the whole school and is not just a reflection of library priorities.

The improvement planning process will involve:

- consultation with senior management about key improvement priorities for the whole school
- consultation with users and non-users about library improvement priorities, including data from the evaluation process (see Chapter 9)
- definition of goals, objectives and desired outcomes linked to priorities and the identification of success criteria
- assessment of the current position of the library, making reference to self-evaluation undertaken, audit of inputs against national guidance and an honest appraisal of current activities
- identification of development actions to deliver defined outcomes
- analysis of any professional development needs of school library staff or partners
- analysis of the financial implications of development
- indication of the timeframe within which the objectives will be achieved
- development of key partnerships, internal and external to the school
- implementation and monitoring (including performance measures to be used); targets need to be SMART (Specific, Measurable, Attainable, Relevant, Time-bound)
- evaluation and communication of the impact of development to staff and students (including appropriate key performance indicators to demonstrate progress against the objectives).

Stakeholder involvement in policy and plan development

The school librarian needs to employ a number of strategies to ensure that library policies and improvement plans accurately reflect the needs of stakeholders and are supported by the whole school community and the school's senior management.

The library committee

Views on the effectiveness of library committees vary. Librarians need to use their professional judgement as to whether this could be a useful tool within the context of their school setting. Committees should be led by the school librarian and may be established to support the development of the library either on a long-term basis or with a fixed-term project focus. Either way it is necessary that they have the full support of senior management and a membership that reflects the interests of the whole school community, including:

- senior management
- the governing body or board of directors
- senior teachers or departmental representatives
- users and non-users – both staff and students.

The library committee can have an important role in planning and winning support for a library policy, as well as offering a channel of communication. It demonstrates that the school library is owned as a whole-school resource and is at the heart of learning and teaching within the school. Where meeting physically is not possible, perhaps owing to the time constraints on teachers, then a virtual library committee could be consulted via e-mail. Its role remains the same, to obtain views from across the school on 'library issues' and to feed back to colleagues any decisions made. This approach means that if an issue is so important that it requires a face-to-face meeting then its very nature will help ensure attendance rather than a termly 'library focused' meeting.

User consultation

It is advisable to consult frequently with users and non-users about what they want from the school library in order to ensure that the library delivers its services effectively. Focus groups, interactive exhibitions and displays, consultations with teachers and students, qualitative as well as quantitative information, user and non-user surveys and informal conversations all provide useful evidence to inform improvement planning. It is important that the school library publicizes action prompted by the findings of consultation. This increases staff and students' ownership of the library and encourages them to participate in future consultation. Qualitative and quantitative evidence-gathering and methods of consultation are dealt with more fully in Chapter 9.

Policy and improvement plan endorsement

In order to win recognition and support for the school library it is important that the policy and the improvement plan are communicated to the senior management team and the governors or board of directors. Student councils also need to know about and support plans for library development. They can be informed via meetings, PowerPoint presentations, displays, written reports, school newspapers, video recordings, podcasts or bulletins. Advocates, such as library-link governors, can also help promote awareness of the results of consultations, evaluations and plans for development. The VLE and school website can promote any changes made, using, for example, 'What you said and what we did' news reports.

4

The library environment

CILIP recommends that the environment of the school library supports its role as a whole-school learning resource. This means that:

- the library is a central resource, accessible and welcoming to all members of the school community
- the library accommodates at least one class
- the library is designed for flexibility to allow a variety of functions
- the design of the library enhances the users' experience and encourages a positive attitude to learning
- the organization of the library is obvious to users of all abilities.

Introduction

While the modern school library extends beyond its four walls, its physical design and layout will set the tone for the environment and ethos of the facility and contribute to the positive experiences of all users: students, staff and the wider school community. As one of the major learning spaces within a school, it must meet the needs of all user groups. The implications of the Equality Act 2010 have been considered throughout this chapter (The Stationery Office, 2010). The following areas, all of which need consideration when planning and managing the library facility, will be looked at:

- location
- size
- design
- use

- signage
- display.

The checklist in Appendix 10 addresses further practical considerations. It is intended to be a tool to help librarians identify the strengths and weaknesses in their existing facilities and plan for improvements. Regardless of the existing space and position of the school library, the majority of general principles outlined here can be applied and are certainly important when planning any new development. School library services, where available, provide an independent, unbiased source of advice and support to the librarian and the school in developing effective and well planned library facilities, and should be consulted in any new development.

Location

The location of the library has an impact on its use. Where new developments are planned or where relocation opportunities arise, the following principles should be taken into account:

1 The library should be on one floor only, preferably the ground floor, to enable good access for disabled users and easy delivery of goods. Where dual school/community use is planned, especially out of school hours, a ground floor location close to an external entrance is essential for security reasons.
2 The library should be centrally sited within the school, close to the maximum number of teaching areas, though not a thoroughfare. An isolated location or separate building will deter regular use.

Size

Immediate change in available space is not possible for most school libraries. However, where a new building or expansion is being considered, recommendations are given below. In all cases it is advised that senior managers are made aware of these recommendations in order to plan for future developments.

The Department for Education and Skills (2004) made recommendations on space requirements in schools, including recommendations for 'learning resource areas', and recognized that the single largest element of these will be the school library. It recommended that school libraries should be able to seat 10% of a school's students at any one time. In practice it is crucial that the library space accommodates a whole class comfortably. Staffing levels in terms of student supervision will determine the practicality of spaces larger than this. In addition, there should be adequate space for library materials, furniture and equipment.

The demands of the curriculum require the library to have adequate space and facilities because:

- the most efficient and cost-effective organization of school resources is in a central collection, rather than scattered in departments, ensuring they are accessible to all
- study table spaces need to be generous enough to accommodate collaborative working practices
- the importance of electronic resources means that there needs to be sufficient space for students to lay out books and other resources and to work together whilst using workstations
- where special collections such as careers information, staff CPD resources, archives and Sixth Form collections are provided in the library for central, open access they need adequate space and shelving to accommodate the variety of formats.

Table 4.1 shows the minimum space recommendations for schools without a Sixth Form. Schools with a Sixth Form should add the space recommendations in Table 4.2 to those in Table 4.1 to work out the recommended space

Table 4.1 Recommended *minimum* library space for an 11–16 school (based on Department for Education and Skills, 2004 figures): $75m^2 + 0.25m^2$ per student in the school	
Number of 11–16 students	**Minimum library accommodation, m^2**
400	175
600	225
800	275
1000	325
1200	375
1400	425
1600	475
1800	525
2000	575

Table 4.2 Additional space requirements for schools with a Sixth Form (based on Department for Education and Skills, 2004, figures): 50m² + 0.45m² per Sixth Form student	
Number of Sixth Form students	**Minimum *additional* library accommodation, m²**
50	72.5
100	95
150	117.5
200	140
250	162.5
300	185
350	207.5
400	230
450	252.5
500	275

for their library. Some schools may choose to include the Sixth Form space within a single large library, others may opt to create quiet work rooms or an entirely separate Sixth Form library, depending on available space, staffing and the needs of the school.

Design

The design of the library needs to allow for a range of uses and access to a large range of resources that are crucial to the teaching and learning programmes of all departments. Classes should regularly visit the library to undertake research with both print and electronic resources, and information literacy skills should be taught and practised. In addition, individuals and small groups should be welcome to drop in to find information or reading material or to pursue a variety of independent learning activities. Large numbers of students will also need to use the library to do their homework, to read, and to find material to further their own individual interests before and after school and at break and lunchtimes.

Layout

A library is a learning space, and the planning and design must focus on this as its principal purpose. However, as a variety of different types of learning may take place in the library, sometimes simultaneously, consideration should be given to providing zoned spaces within the library for different purposes. These may include:

- a working area for a whole class
- a space for individual tutoring or small group work
- a comfortable, informal area for leisure reading
- a quiet study area.

The arrangement of fiction and non-fiction resources should take into account the expected use of the materials. The location of any desktop computers in the library should allow for easy staff oversight and variations in use. Consideration must be given to the use of laptops and other electronic devices for which access to plug-in points or the wireless network will be needed. In any planning of the arrangement of furniture, care must be taken to allow sufficient floor space for safe movement of students and to ensure that the access of disabled students and staff is not restricted.

Lighting

The level of lighting can affect how students perform. Light that is too bright can make some learners restless and fidgety and cause difficulties for students with particular sight problems. Some students find that low light has a calming effect and enables them to think more clearly. However, care must be taken to ensure that lighting is sufficiently bright to maintain safety and allow all students to access the resources without impairing their vision. Variation in lighting levels can be created in different areas of the library with careful positioning of spotlights, wall-mounted light-fittings and study lamps.

Heating

Since some learners need warmth in order to study while others prefer cool temperatures, it is vital to ensure that the learning environment is adequately ventilated. The Health and Safety Executive requires a minimum working temperature of at least 16°C and their advice on thermal comfort states that where regular complaints are received about the level of heat, measures such as shaded windows, pipe insulation and air-cooling systems should be installed (Health and Safety Executive, n.d.). It is recommended that, where necessary, the problem of excessive temperatures should be raised with the school's health and safety representative.

Colour

Careful thought needs to be given to colour choices and combinations. A study of the effect of colour on learning found that cool colours, such as blue, green, violet and grey, are beneficial to concentration, and that pale, neutral colours such as cream or magnolia are recommended for large wall areas within learning spaces (Engelbrecht, 2003). Splashes of deeper colour are important in breaking up monotony and these can be introduced through effective signage and display, which is discussed later in this chapter.

Safety of movement

The school library differs from a classroom in that students are likely to be moving around the room on a regular basis, locating a variety of resources or sharing and swapping ideas. Purposeful movement within the library is to be encouraged and the expectation should be that working students are able to move around the room as necessary. The arrangement of furniture should be such that safe movement is possible at all times and consideration should be given to where students will store items such as bags and coats to ensure that they do not form a trip hazard, particularly for students and staff with disabilities.

Staff working area

The requirement for administrative and office space should not be overlooked. It should include storage space, shelving, staff desk(s) and computer(s), and a filing cabinet and work area for processing new acquisitions, and it should have a good visual overview of the library.

The issue desk has long been accepted as an essential focal point of a library. However, it can be imposing and it can separate the library staff from the users. Librarians should consider whether the traditional model is still useful, particularly in situations where self-issue systems are installed. Whatever configuration is decided upon, be it a multi-functional desk that includes space for administrative activities, or a small enquiry point, it is essential that the design and height do not impair access for users with disabilities or present a barrier to effective interaction with any user.

Use

The way the school library is used is crucial to its ability to achieve its optimum contribution to the school. This cannot be achieved where the library is timetabled for use as an ordinary classroom, or negatively used as a detention area, a Sixth Form social area, or a place to send badly behaved, unsupervised students. There is a need to create a design that actively promotes a learning ethos for all students and an attractive, welcoming environment plays a large part in making the library a valued and well used part of the school.

Many librarians involve students in the design, furnishing and rule-setting of the library which can be a powerful way of encouraging their ownership and pride in the facility. The use of the library should be part of wider discussions about the general ethos of the school and is likely to included factors such as:

- noise
- eating and drinking
- acceptable and expected standards of behaviour.

Noise

Many students are so used to music or noisy environments that they do not notice the noise around them and can work well in a noisy environment and some may find some level of background noise beneficial to learning. Conversely, there will always be some students who need quiet to concentrate and work effectively. The learning environment of the library should cater for all. Dependent on space and the number of students using the library, this could be achieved by having a quiet study room, a zoned 'quiet working' area, or having quiet times during the day. Students for whom discussion is important will often need to talk with other learners and provision should be made for this too, either in zoned areas or at particular times of the day, depending on the needs of the specific school community.

Some school libraries use a sound system for soft background classical music for downtime and reflection. The use of headphones within the library to allow students to listen to music while they work provides another solution. However, any use of music within the library should not be done in isolation from the overarching policies of the rest of the school.

Eating and drinking

A decision on the advisability of allowing this in the library will depend on local circumstances and should be left to the librarian.

Behaviour

The type of behaviour that is acceptable in the library is likely to reflect the ethos of the rest of the school. However, in some cases the library may be seen as slightly different to other areas in terms of behaviour. For example:

- In a school which has difficulties with student behaviour around the site the expectation of acceptable behaviour in the library may be higher than in other parts of the school, in order to create a safe and secure haven for students.
- In a school with very formal expectations of behaviour in classrooms and corridors the library may have a more tolerant attitude to the type of behaviour that is accepted in order to create a more relaxed atmosphere for developing students' personal reading interests and independent learning skills.

Any deviation from the standard practice of the school in terms of acceptable behaviour should be agreed with the school's senior leadership and governors and should be fully justified in terms of safety and learning. In addition, library staff should expect to have access to the school's rewards and sanctions for good and bad behaviour, in line with teaching staff.

Encouraging students to get involved in setting acceptable rules for use can be beneficial in fostering a sense of ownership and helping students to understand the need for rules. However, where this is done it is important to involve a wide range of students, otherwise the area can be seen as belonging to one particular sector of the school community, leaving others feeling excluded. The emphasis of any behaviour rules and guidelines for the library should always be based on:

- the safety of the students and staff in the library
- the function of the library as a learning space
- the creation of an environment that is welcoming to as many students, staff and other members of the school community as possible.

Signage

Good signage is essential both inside and outside the library, including clear signposting from other parts of the school. Students should be consulted as to the types of signs needed to guide them to the locations and resources they need. Within the library, consideration should be given to:

- a plan of the library
- bay or ceiling and shelf guides to indicate non-fiction subjects and fiction genre or author areas
- a subject index that leads into full subject access through the library catalogue
- guidelines and notices about the use of the library, including copyright and acceptable behaviour.

Notices should be phrased positively (e.g. 'Please take your food and snacks to the areas of the school where eating is allowed' rather than 'Please don't eat or drink in the library').

All main signs should be pictorial, with a minimum of text, so as not to exclude students with special needs. Text which is all in caps should be avoided, as it is more difficult to read. Consideration should be given to signs in community languages as well. All signs should be designed with clarity for external visitors and for people with physical, including visual, disabilities. More advice on this is available from the British Dyslexia Association (n.d.).

Display

Display is not only a powerful tool for the promotion of library resources, services and activities but also for enhancing the literacy of students and stimulating their intellectual curiosity. Everything should be designed with this in mind. Displays should always be up to date, often designed in collaboration with students and possibly focused on some of the following:

- students' work resulting from library activities such as book reviews and projects
- promotion and information about new acquisitions
- resources on chosen themes or interests
- stories in the news linked to relevant library resources
- general information about events and activities in the library, the school and the local community.

Display is particularly important to visual learners. Brightly coloured display boards can be used not only to showcase outstanding student work, but also as an interactive resource. For example, a scribble board can be used for posing questions, suggesting answers and putting forward ideas for discussion, or a word wall can be created for students to add their own definitions, encouraging students to extend their vocabulary.

Display systems are available from all major library and school suppliers. These include wall-mounted and portable display boards, leaflet dispensers, book stands and end display panels for shelving units. Alternatively, card-based display board (e.g. Kappa-board) can be purchased locally from specialist art suppliers, cut to size and painted or covered with paper to provide attractive backgrounds for displays.

5

Management of learning resources

CILIP recommends that the school supports the vital role that sufficient quality resources play in stimulating learning and maximizes the impact of this investment by managing resources centrally. This means that:

- all members of the school community have equal access to the library services
- resources are recorded centrally
- the stock selection policy aims to provide for the needs of all users
- funding is sufficient to provide enough up-to-date and relevant resources to meet users' needs.

Introduction

The complexity of managing learning resources has grown considerably in the last few years with the expansion of electronic information and e-resources available to schools. This chapter offers guidance on managing this growth by examining the issues of:

- needs assessment
- budgeting
- selection
- location
- organization and access.

The current context for managing learning resources is characterized by:

- an emphasis on independent learning

- the recognition of the importance of independent reading in the development of literacy
- the unique contribution to reader development made by the library
- the key importance of information literacy
- the use of ICT as a tool for teaching and learning
- the importance of e-learning and the development of intranets, websites and virtual learning environments (VLEs)
- the growing availability of mobile devices as a point of access to information
- an awareness of social inequalities in access to high-quality information
- an increased understanding of how the brain works – the physiology of learning.

Students should enjoy using the library's resources. They need to see their own interests and cultures reflected and validated by inclusion in the school library. The best resources collections will inspire an enthusiasm to learn, stimulate curiosity and suit a variety of learning styles. This means that the secondary school library must contain a full range of imaginative fiction, from picture books to teen fiction to adult novels, and the widest possible non-fiction range. It needs to include representations of different life styles, cultures (including youth culture) and faiths. Resources need to relate directly to curriculum needs to support and sustain students' achievement and provision should also be made for quality resources supporting students wider interests. Access to electronic resources needs to be integrated with books, recordings and resources provided in other media. The richer the resource base, the richer the learning experience of students.

Librarians need to be clear about the cost implications of these demands. Senior managers need to be kept informed so that they can ensure that they are financed accordingly, and that the human resources necessary to manage them effectively are in place.

Needs assessment

In order to build a relevant resource base for the whole school community, librarians should be involved in a continuous process of needs assessment, comparing changing demands to available resources. This process forms the foundation for planning collection development and budget requests. In brief, librarians need to:

- maintain a constant awareness of curriculum changes and developments both internally and in the national arena
- be aware of priorities in the school improvement plan and ensure that the resources reflect these targets
- be aware of trends and developments in children and young people's fiction
- keep up to date with developments in online and digital resources
- involve students and staff by encouraging them to recommend purchases
- ensure that the stock is accessible to all levels of ability to enable differentiation
- have a knowledge of how access to learning resources can be provided for users who have special needs or who are disabled
- use data from school-wide assessments of students' home access to information technology, including broadband internet and printing facilities, in order to ensure that resources are available in formats which meet the needs of the whole-school community
- be familiar with the physical, emotional and moral issues facing young people and manage resources relating to these issues in a supportive way
- be aware of issues of cultural diversity both within the school and in the wider community
- be aware of changes in the make-up of the school community, such as changes to intake or local demographics, which could cause changes in the demands on resources
- have knowledge of and be able to assess resources available from external sources such as the school library service, local public libraries, museums and archives, and the British Library, and be able to judge the cost-effectiveness of accessing these resources in relation to the demand within the school
- carry out regular, systematic stock checks and regular reviews and evaluation of stock, including purchased online resources, to measure relevance to existing demands and to ensure that plans for future developments are based on evidence of recent trends in resource use.

Budgeting

The annual library improvement plan is the appropriate place to highlight collection development needs and the financial commitment required to meet them, as discussed in Chapter 3. The development of bids for resources funding should include:

- consultation with senior management to identify whole-school priorities in the school improvement plan
- liaison with curriculum managers and subject teachers to determine curriculum needs and changes
- the monitoring of student and teacher needs via suggestions, surveys, and statistics of use
- assessing the resource implications of Ofsted or other inspection reports
- comparison of current stock, including online subscriptions, against recommended levels and identified needs
- providing a rationale for granting additional funding within the library budget for the purchase of online resources rather than funding online resources for whole-school use from central funds. Where online resources are funded centrally the librarian should be involved in the selection process
- reviewing stock to plan for filling gaps and replacing outdated and worn materials
- review of school library service provision and the appropriate level of support, where available
- calculation of costs of proposals based on current average unit costs, student numbers, recommended stock figures and inflation, obsolescence, withdrawal and replacement
- preparing cogent, well supported and documented presentations to senior management.

The budget bid will need to be submitted to senior leadership or to the governors in accordance with school procedures. The emphasis for budget setting should always be on meeting the identified resource needs of the school and its students.

Recommended figures for library resourcing

In the previous edition of these guidelines (Barrett and Douglas, 2004) CILIP recommended that:

- libraries stock a minimum of 13 items per student in the 11–14 age group and 17 items per student in the 14–19 age group
- the ratio of fiction to non-fiction may vary from 1:4 to 1:5
- 10% of the stock be replaced annually.

These figures still hold true for a traditional school library but so much material has become available electronically that in practice the picture is now a lot less clear-cut. Today, much depends on the level of access to quality online resources, the needs and types of users and the priorities of the school. For example, 11–14-year-olds may need more paper resources than older students because selecting and using the majority of online resources appropriately requires more developed reading and information literacy competencies.

CILIP recommends that:

- **The physical stock, e.g. books, magazines and DVDs, are in excellent condition, relevant to the needs of the users and up to date. This will be maintained by an average stock replacement of around 10% per year.**
- **The school library has a wide and varied stock that includes books (electronic, paper or audio), magazines, online subscriptions, DVDs and newspapers. The exact ratios will reflect the professional judgement of the librarian in the light of school priorities and library usage.**

Budgeting exemplars are available in Appendix 6 and cover the cost of setting up a new library and the approximate yearly running costs.

Selection

A key responsibility of the librarian is to meet identified student and staff needs with quality information and fiction resources. This depends on good communication between librarians and all sectors of the school population, as well as the librarian's professional knowledge of the curriculum, publishing and external sources of information.

Resource policy

A written resource policy, where there is one, will include:

- criteria for the identification and selection of books, newspapers and magazines, multimedia and e-resources, including internet sites made accessible through the library system, or the school's intranet, website or virtual learning environment (VLE)
- criteria for comparing the cost-effectiveness of different information formats, including local usage patterns as well as an awareness of the impact of licensing agreements, the cost of annual subscriptions and the expected life span of the resource
- the need for current, accurate and authoritative materials
- the need for materials that promote reading for pleasure, both fiction and non-fiction, ensuring a broad collection of fiction covering a wide range of genres and styles to enable students to read classic and contemporary authors for pleasure, to improve literacy and to develop an understanding of the literary heritage
- the need for materials reflecting curriculum development
- the need for materials covering leisure interests
- an appropriate balance between fiction and non-fiction
- materials in alternative formats that are accessible to visually impaired library users and those with other special needs
- differentiated materials in a variety of formats appropriate to the ability range and interests of the students, enabling access and stimulation for all
- materials in a range of formats that take into account levels of individual access to online resources, printing facilities and e-book platforms within the school population
- materials in community languages
- materials balanced to avoid sexist, cultural, political, ethical or homophobic bias
- materials reflecting current youth culture and concerns
- procedures for assessing and managing donated resources
- clearly worded guidance on any restrictions the school may place on open access to resources, such as age-restricted collections or requirements for parental permission for access to online resources
- clear procedures for handling complaints.

Aids to selection

Aids to selection include:

- encouraging students and staff to participate in selection and to offer comments and suggestions
- enabling students to help with stock selection through shop and library supplier visits, by using the internet and social media and by reading reviews
- encouraging students or members of the community with specific language skills to participate in the selection of materials in these languages
- keeping up to date with quality, unbiased, critical information about new resources across all formats in the professional press and on the internet
- accessing the expertise of school library service staff, where available, for advice and information about the latest publications
- attending exhibitions of resources held at major library suppliers or school library services and at major library and education exhibitions
- taking advantage of visits from publishers' representatives or booksellers, bearing in mind that it is important to ensure that any 'bargain' boxes of books are good value for money and genuinely meet the library's most pressing resource needs
- participating in local consortia for the purchase of electronic resources
- collaborating in school policy-setting relating to restrictions on and freedom of access to online resources.

In addition to fiction and non-fiction collections, the library may also include some special collections where appropriate, such as careers and life-skills materials, professional resources for staff, local studies resources and relevant community information. In some schools these items may be kept in a different place and organized by someone with relevant specialist knowledge, for example the Sixth Form Manager or Careers Co-ordinator, who is highly skilled in this area.

Schools should be aware that, whilst the internet contains a vast array of useful information available to students with appropriate information literacy skills, it must be emphasized that student access to the free internet, with its increasing volume of opinion and crowd-sourced information, is an addition to and not a substitute for reviewed and carefully selected information resources. Some librarians will select and promote appropriate websites via their library management system's computer catalogue.

Location

The convenience of individual teachers or departments has to be weighed against the financial and educational benefits of having a central resource when making decisions about the location of resources:

1 The widest possible range of resources needs to be available, in one location, for students and staff to access when they need them.
2 The school network and the internet need to be available in the library with access sufficient for at least half the school's largest class to use at any one time.
3 The establishment of permanent pocket collections of resources in departments may result in high levels of loss and costly duplications between departments. Wherever possible, resources should be based in the library and recorded on the library management system for ease of location and to facilitate use by the whole school.
4 Where resources need to be held in departments for lengthy periods these should be issued to the department as a loan and responsibility for the safekeeping of the materials should rest with the department in which they are stored.

Organization and access

Providing clear, unfettered access to a collection is the single most important factor in maximizing its effectiveness and stimulating use. *The School Library Manifesto* (IFLA/UNESCO, 2000) says 'Access to services and collections should be based on the United Nations Universal Declaration of Human Rights and Freedoms, and should not be subject to any form of ideological, political or religious censorship, or to commercial pressures.' Nevertheless, while libraries need to be orderly and systematic, they also need to be flexible in the presentation of materials. Children learn in different ways and the emphasis should be on how students will be drawn to resources and how they will use them. Generally speaking, this will mean:

- organizing non-fiction using the Dewey Decimal System
- arranging fiction by genre or author (where the school operates any form of graded reading scheme it is recommended that fiction within the scheme is still arranged by genre or author in order to encourage students to develop a familiarity with these concepts and to be able to facilitate their progression to the more independent selection of reading material)
- central recording of all learning resources in the school on the library management system; this will enable staff and students to have easy access to materials and provides for cost efficient measures to be taken, such as textbook issues and departmental stock checks
- online access to the library management system for students and staff in order to facilitate independent use through the location, selection and reservation of resources both in and outside of the school
- flexibility in order to spark interest as part of a promotion or to make materials more accessible in a particular local situation
- comprehensive and accurate key-wording of all materials, including recommended internet sites and other e-resources, in the library management system, which will lead students directly to resources, regardless of location, and encourage them to value all types of sources in their research; this includes linking resource access via the library pages on the school's intranet, website or VLE
- printed subject indexes, posters, directional signage or leaflets and bookmarks that point students quickly to a general section and which may form part of the library's promotion and display
- clear resource- and shelf-labelling linked to the details in the library management system that encourage students to develop independence in locating resources for themselves
- guidance signposting aimed at encouraging critical thinking in the selection and use of internet sites; further details on information literacy skills are contained in Chapter 6
- liaison with teaching staff to enable the promotion of the resources in lessons and remotely through the website or VLE.

6

Information literacy

CILIP recommends that the librarian takes a lead role in the development of students' information literacy skills to enable all students to become independent, lifelong learners. This means that:

- there is a whole-school approach to information literacy, with the librarian and all subject teachers using an agreed model and language
- information literacy skills are seen as important at every key stage, to establish good habits and develop higher level skills
- the school recognizes the librarian's professional expertise in information retrieval and knowledge of plagiarism issues and expects staff to collaborate in making best use of these.

Information literacy in the 21st century

The challenge that we face in the 21st century, more than ever before, is knowing how to satisfy our information needs with information that is reliable. Information literacy (IL) is a term used to encompass the skills and competencies that are required for navigating the information explosion that technology has unleashed. There are many challenges and decisions that are faced by consumers of information today. Information is available through an ever-increasing range of media that can be accessed purposely or casually by browsing or by following links. There are many reasons that motivate individuals to find information, ranging from education and work to fun and entertainment. In addition, all consumers have to make ethical decisions about how they use the material that they find in relation to issues such as plagiarism and copyright (Webber, 2010). These components link together to form the why and how of 21st-century information-seeking behaviour. With 24-hour access to information sources this process of information consumption is on-going. Information literacy skills cannot be ignored; they are an educational imperative and a 'basic human right in a digital world' which promote 'social inclusion in all nations' (IFLA, 2005). Figure 6.1 summarizes 21st-century information-seeking behaviour.

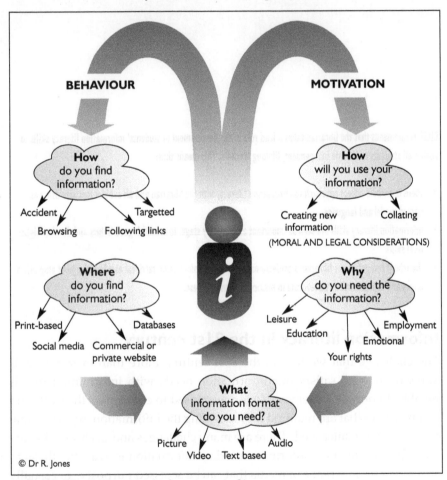

Figure 6.1 Why and how we seek information in the 21st century

Key information literacy definitions

Information literacy skills are recognized both nationally and internationally. In the UK, the leading professional body for information, library and knowledge practitioners defines information literacy as 'knowing when and why you need information, where to find it, and how to evaluate, use and communicate it in an ethical manner' (CILIP, 2013b). IFLA (2013) quotes the American Library Association, saying 'To be information literate, a person must be able to recognize when information is needed and have the ability to locate, evaluate and use effectively the needed information'. Information literacy is a global concern. Information-literate citizens are more able to make informed decisions and therefore improve their own lives and the society in which they live.

Information literacy (IL) skills in schools

The Demos report (Bartlett and Miller, 2011) revealed that although 'digital natives' (12–18-year-olds) were confident users of technology, the majority of them did not apply good judgement when selecting information sources and websites. The report notes that:

- too many digital natives do not apply checks to the information they access
- aesthetics are valued over quality
- there is a lack of teaching.

The report uses the term 'digital fluency' to describe the skills and knowledge needed to 'find and critically evaluate online information'. It emphasizes that all children need to be able to 'search, retrieve, contextualize, analyse, visualize and synthesize information effectively' and that these skills are fundamental.

Information literacy skills need to be taught and students need supporting in this process. As with every skill, IL skills need to be revisited, developed and practised. This means they cannot simply be taught in Year 7. Opportunities need to be built in across the range of curriculum subjects so that students have to apply their skills in different contexts and situations across the key stages.

Terminology and skills definitions

CILIP (2013b) states that for students to handle and process information successfully, they need to be able to:

1 **Question**. Identify a problem, establish what is already known and frame questions around what is not known, or that which may be believed without firm evidence.
2 **Plan**. Devise a plan for taking enquiries forward and completing a research task.
3 **Identify and evaluate sources**. Establish appropriate search strategies, identify appropriate sources of information and analyse and evaluate the information found.
4 **Analyse and organize key information**. Compare and contrast information identifying key ideas and concepts and make appropriate notes and records using a variety of techniques. Discard what is not needed and organize the relevant information and document sources.
5 **Synthesize and assimilate**. Combine relevant information from a variety of sources into a new whole. Compare with what was already known and assimilate new understandings or decisions, building new knowledge networks in the process.
6 **Reflect**. Revisit questions and test for any gaps to see if supporting information is sufficient to enable a conclusion to be drawn or a decision to be made.
7 **Communicate**. Communicate the new learning or the conclusion to the intended audience in an appropriate way, with insight, detail and accuracy in an effective, original presentation.
8 **Evaluate**. Evaluate the final product and the whole learning process to complete the task, drawing conclusions about what has been learned and the effectiveness of the process.

The need for these skills is not new. Bloom (1956) identified them in his Taxonomy, where the differentiation between lower-order cognitive skills (knowledge, comprehension, application) and higher-order cognitive skills (analysis, synthesis, evaluation) is articulated. Marland then developed his 9 Question Steps (LISC, 1984), from which further models evolved in the 1980s and 1990s. Some widely used ones are:

- The Big6 (Eisenberg and Berkovitz, 1990), http://big6.com
- PLUS Model (Herring, 1999)
- Exit Model (Wray and Lewis, 1995).

Developing the provision of information literacy skills

The development of information literacy skills can be achieved through change that is driven by senior leaders or through change that is developed by middle leaders, with the librarian and individual subject teachers collaborating on projects. For information literacy skills to be successfully integrated throughout the school, senior leaders and teachers need to be on board. This is difficult to achieve, as often both educational and institutional barriers will need to be overcome. Teachers are under pressure to deliver subject content to ensure that students fulfil their exam grade potential, and courses are designed so that students can largely rely on textbooks and hand-outs as their primary sources of information. Teaching staff may need support in order to start facilitating independence in their students.

Vision

It is crucial that the librarian is able to communicate a coherent overall vision to colleagues. If the librarian wants to see information literacy teaching shared across all staff, who then set guided tasks that involve students searching and retrieving information based on a chosen model, then staff need to be convinced of the benefits of teaching information literacy skills. The librarian will need to take a lead if information literacy is to become embedded into lesson planning, teacher assessments and schemes of work. Every school has key documents, such as the improvement plan or Ofsted or ISI reports, that outline its vision and direction. Sections aimed at improving standards of teaching and learning, student attainment levels and utilization of ICT and new technology all provide the librarian with an opportunity for advocating the benefits of teaching information literacy skills.

The educational rationale for teaching information literacy skills

It is important to show how information literacy skills link to educational priorities such as literacy, digital literacy, e-safety and citizenship. Referring to existing initiatives may demonstrate the value that other organizations place on information literacy. Education Scotland (2013) has a dedicated section on its education website that focuses on Information and Critical Literacy and provides a collection of accessible learning materials. The draft

National Information Literacy Framework (Scotland) (Irving and Crawford, 2007) details the expected skill levels for students in schools. The Welsh Information Project (Welsh Libraries, 2009) is another initiative that clearly links IL skills and educational goals.

Information literacy skills teaching:

1 **Develops thinking skills.** Students develop their questioning skills. They need to identify exactly what they need to know and then choose the most appropriate sources, be that a subject-based source or a social media site that matches the task. They need to factor in bias and motivation of the author before engaging with the ideas and presenting them in the most relevant form for their intended audience.

2 **Encourages lifelong learning.** Individuals are empowered to engage with society in a confident and effective manner. Students learn skills that enable them to take control of their learning and use strategies to problem-solve, engage with technology and critically analyse their information-seeking strategies. These skills stimulate the desire for learning that can continue beyond formal educational settings.

3 **Raises literacy standards.** Students are taught reading strategies (skimming, scanning, intensive reading) and critical reading (reading for a purpose) that can be applied to a variety of different resources, which enable them to choose the most effective approach for their own reading.

4 **Supports differentiation.** Information literacy skills incorporate a variety of techniques for finding and processing information. This allows students to practise a range of strategies and determine which ones work best for them.

5 **Develops the effective use of ICT and supports online safety teaching.** Students are required to manage, organize and collate information and information sources. Apps are available to support students in their development of information literacy skills and some websites and blogs provide links to the range of iPad and Android apps that are available (e.g. Shrock, 2011; Kharbach, 2012). Enabling students to use search engines effectively and to understand how and when to use collaborative material such as Wikipedia equips them with the knowledge and understanding that leads them to do more than simply 'Google' for everything. This results in a greater appreciation of the value of information and encourages the questioning of 'free' sources. By helping

students to exercise good judgement online and evaluate the websites they use through better questioning and analysing skills, it supports in-school online safety teaching and encourages individuals to be aware of the personal details they share when accessing information and signing up to online sources.

6 **Enhances students' ability to explore the national curricula.** Students who can question information, analyse and reflect, allow teaching to be more student-led and teachers to deliver their subjects in a more student-centred manner.

7 **Enables students to understand the concept of plagiarism.** Plagiarism is a whole-school concern. Information literacy skills equip both teaching staff and students with a knowledge of both how and why they need to cite references and create a bibliography to support their fact-finding, opinions and arguments. Understanding the behaviours that constitute plagiarism can lead to an improvement in academic practice throughout the school.

From planning into action

If changes are to be introduced, then a written plan is needed that details what, how, when and with whom. The stages below will need to be worked through:

1 **Linking the information literacy skills plan to the:**
   - school improvement plan
   - library improvement plan
   - subject improvement plans (writing the collaboration or project into the library plan in the first instance, with the aim of getting the library included in the subsequent subject improvement plan)
   - schemes of work by agreement with the relevant member of staff.
2 **Identification of the target group(s):**
   - an individual class
   - a key stage
   - a year group(s)
   - particular subjects
   - individual teachers.
3 **Aims and outcomes agreed with relevant teaching staff.** It is

important to meet with teaching staff to identify the outcomes that it is hoped the plan will achieve and how they are to be measured:
- what skills will students learn or develop?
- how will student progress or development be measured?
- what topic is suitable?
- when will the project take place?
- how long will the students need to process new skills, access and process new information?
- how will the librarian work with the class?
- what will be the librarian's role in evaluating the product?
- what materials need preparing?
- lesson planning and format
- ICT booking.

4   **Plan.** Draw up an agreed plan with the teacher and agree the methods for measuring success. These may be IL-based and specific to the students' achievement or some may be linked to the integration of IL teaching into lessons. Some suggested outcomes are listed below:

Information literacy-based outcomes:
- students have used specified databases to retrieve 3 relevant sources
- students have produced annotated bibliographies
- 50% of students demonstrated the use of advance search techniques
- 70% of students used websites that they had located on the library catalogue.

Integration of information literacy outcomes:
- the collaborative lessons are written into schemes of work
- the librarian has a defined role in the marking of student work from an information literacy skills perspective
- the lessons are formally reviewed and evaluated by both the librarian and the teacher.

5   **Resources.** When planning to deliver IL skills it is important to have a selection of reliable and up-to-date online resources that can provide a first port of call for students and staff. To ensure value for money, joining a local consortium, such as JCS (2013), allows schools to purchase subscriptions at a discount. Another option is harnessing the resources that are available via the public library. These will include general reference databases and newspaper databases. The librarian should prepare the relevant resources. This could range from assembling a book

box and cataloguing websites to devising a database research guide and identifying relevant social media.

6   **Deliver or support the lessons.** This could involve the librarian in leading the session, supporting the teacher or a combination of both of these options. It can be useful to describe the librarian as the skills expert and the class teacher as the subject expert. Notes taken at the time will be useful aids to accurately reflecting on the experience.

7   **Evaluate.** The librarian should evaluate the student outcomes/product with the class teacher. This could mean viewing a presentation, assessing the range of sources used or how information has been integrated into the work.

8   **Review the lessons from the librarian's perspective**:
   • were the outcomes achieved?
   • did the lessons go to plan?
   • what can be learned from the experience?

9   **Review the lessons from the teacher's perspective**:
   • what were the teacher's experiences of the unit of work or project?
   • what did they think of student performance and outcomes?
   • what changes would they make?

10   **Repeat /modify/abandon.** After evaluating the plan, a decision needs to be made as to whether it was successful enough to repeat or if a new strategy is required.

11   **Liaise with the head of department to write the lessons/project into the scheme of work.** This ensures that collaboration will continue and that inclusion of the joint project is not dependent on a particular teacher.

Developing information literacy skills

Information literacy skills need to be built upon if students are to become proficient. Once a skill has been taught, students need opportunities to develop and master it so that it becomes part of their information-seeking and evaluating behaviour. This is why it is important that successful projects are written into schemes of work.

Information literacy skills, like all other skills, have the most impact on learning when they are taught, modelled and practised within a meaningful context. Ideally these skills will be introduced in a developmental progression.

In order for this to happen, each step must be carefully coached and supported, as well as differentiated by age and ability levels. It is also important that these steps are seen as a cyclical rather than a linear process in which students reflect upon and refine their strategies as they question, analyse, assimilate, evaluate, conclude and learn.

Staff roles in the delivery of information literacy skills teaching

The development of information literacy skills teaching in school will involve a range of people. Below is a guide to the responsibilities and requirements of different members of the school.

Librarians

Librarians need to:

- be involved with curriculum developments and attend relevant heads of department meetings
- manage and develop a resource base that meets the needs of the students and teaching staff
- be aware of key educational initiatives and their impact on teaching and learning
- collaborate with teaching staff in planning lessons, selecting appropriate activities and assessing students' progress
- understand learning styles and the strategies that help students learn
- gather evidence of information literacy development within the school and support further developments in information literacy
- provide staff INSET sessions and assist teaching staff to disseminate examples of good practice.

Teachers

Teachers need to:

- identify opportunities for information literacy skills teaching
- work with the librarian in planning, differentiating, implementing, and evaluating information literacy teaching embedded in their subjects

- share teaching and learning strategies with the librarian and provide students with opportunities to practise information literacy skills.

Senior managers

Senior managers need to:

- support the development of information literacy skills within the school by providing the librarian with access to support and training
- ensure that the development of the library, its resources, and its role in teaching and learning within the school is part of the development and planning process of the school.

Opportunities for information literacy teaching: inside the curriculum

Some curriculum subjects and exam specifications provide more obvious opportunities for information literacy activities than others. For the librarian, it is often about starting conversations with teaching staff about the information literacy skills opportunities that exist within the teacher's own subject.

An important department to liaise with is ICT. There is often some crossover with information literacy skills and the ICT curriculum, especially with the skills of evaluating sources, organizing information, searching for information and presenting information. ICT lessons also enable students to learn a variety of software tools that could be used in conjunction with information literacy skills. Collaboration with colleagues for events such as Safer Internet Day can highlight the information literacy skills that students require when making judgements about the quality and reliability of online materials and in relation to the ethical use of information.

Technology as a tool

Web 2.0 technology has resulted in a variety of apps that can be used in the delivery of IL skills, and countless more are being developed each week. Most of the tools encourage user collaboration and require students to make decisions about the best choice of information sources. Many basic versions of the software are free to the user, with the more advanced features requiring payment or subscriptions. Some services also have specific education accounts that ensure online safety for student users. Some examples of useful tools are outlined below.

Collating information

These tools enable the user to collect websites and web pages and organize them into user-defined groups. Often lists can then be shared. These tools require the user to select information that they deem to be relevant and they provide an instant means of recording the desired information. Discussions with students can then take place around their selection processes. Highlighting the text on a web page so that it is visible to others can stimulate discussion. Tools to try include Diigo, Netvibes and Pinterest. A guide on setting up a Diigo account can be found in the files on the Heart of the School website (http://heartoftheschool.edublogs.org) and an example of a school Netvibes page is given below.

Information updates

Tools such as RSS feed readers enable users to keep up to date with the latest news relating to their own interests and to create a bespoke current awareness service. In schools, this means that students will have to make decisions about the importance of currency in relation to their information need and the reliability and credibility of the updates received. An example of a Netvibes page created by a school librarian for their school can be seen at www.netvibes.com/mplibrary#Eltham_College (permission given).

Social media

Twitter and other social media sites have an ever-increasing influence on how events are reported and ideas are shared. Sites such as Storify (https://storify.com) and Scoop.it (www.scoop.it) enable the curating and archiving of events. A good tutorial on how to use Scoop.it can be found on YouTube at http://youtu.be/oQ4c7khU3J4?t=1m30s. Users can select the voices and opinions that they believe are important and share this construct of an event with others. From archived events, students can explore how ideas develop and can examine the interpretation that can be placed on an event. The difference between the instant reaction to an event and the response to an archived version can then be discussed by students.

Linking

QR codes enable the user to access linked text, pictures or videos through the use of a code reader. Codes are easy to generate and most smart devices have QR code readers that can be easily uploaded. There are many innovative ways to use these codes: they can be physically attached to things or featured on a presentation slide or website page. A QR code that has been created by a librarian could be placed on a book and link the user to a reading list, for example. An excellent slideshare presentation with lots of ways to use QR codes in the classroom or library can be found at http://goo.gl/pCnBal.

Project qualifications

Project qualifications (at Foundation, Higher and Extended levels), the Extended Essay section of the International Baccalaureate and the Pre-U Global Perspectives 'A' level are courses that provide the librarian with an excellent opportunity for teaching and supporting information literacy skills. Each course requires students to undertake independent research, evaluation and critical analysis of information along with the development of project management and planning skills. There is also a strong emphasis on the reviewing process and justifying why certain sources have been chosen and others rejected.

International Baccalaureate Extended Essay

The International Baccalaureate Extended Essay requires students to undertake an extended piece of research that demonstrates evidence of satisfying the following assessment criteria:

Emphasis is placed on the research process:
- formulating an appropriate research question
- engaging in a personal exploration of the topic
- communicating ideas
- developing an argument.

Participation in this process develops the capacity to:

- analyse
- synthesize, and
- evaluate knowledge.

International Baccalaureate, 2005

For the Extended Project Qualification (EPQ) a student must possess a high standard of information literacy skills. Currently two main exam boards offer the project qualifications:

AQA Extended Project Qualification

Our EPQ allows each student to embark on a largely self-directed and self-motivated project. Students must **choose a topic, plan, research and develop their idea** and decide on their finished product.

AQA, 2013

Edexcel Extended Projects

Extended Projects . . . provide opportunities for the development of **critical, reflective, problem-solving and independent learning skills** through the planning, research and evaluation of a self-selected project.

Edexcel, 2013

In some schools librarians have become project supervisors or project co-ordinators as their information literacy skills expertise places them in a strong position to drive these subjects forward. These project-based qualifications model the independent learning skills required of students at undergraduate-level study, and require students to learn and evidence the skills described in the information literacy models outlined above. It is these skills that are the expertise of school librarians, and these qualifications provide a golden opportunity for librarians to not only support, but lead, in the planning of the course, the teaching of the skills, the supervision of students and the marking of final projects. Support and training can be obtained through the exam boards. The School Library Association (2013) also offers an online course that provides the librarian with an understanding of how to support the EPQ and how to develop appropriate library services. Librarians should look at the course specifications and mark schemes to get an insight into the demands of the course, and identify the opportunities that this qualification offers for librarians to take a lead in the teaching and learning of information literacy.

Opportunities for information literacy teaching: outside the curriculum

Teaching IL skills can take place outside of the formal curriculum. The librarian should find out what clubs and societies take place in school and offer to help them with their research, or suggest attending a meeting to provide some tailored information literacy training that focuses on their interest. Debating societies, subject-specific clubs and 'model United Nations' are likely to offer such opportunities.

Sources of further information, good practice and research

ILG	Information Literacy Group (part of CILIP), www.cilip.org.uk/about/special-interest-groups/information-literacy-group.
LILAC	Annual Information Literacy conference run by the ILG.
OFQUAL	Office of Qualifications and Examinations Regulation, www2.ofqual.gov.uk/downloads/category/129-guidance. Download various guides on plagiarism aimed at parents, teachers or students
SID	Safer Internet Day, www.saferinternet.org.uk/safer-internet-day/ 2014.
SLA	School Library Association, www.sla.org.uk.
SLG	School Library Group (part of CILIP), www.cilip.org.uk/about/special-interest-groups/school-libraries-group.

Blogs on information literacy

A New Curriculum for Information Literacy, http://newcurriculum.wordpress.com.
Shelia Webber's Information Literacy weblog, http://information-literacy.blogspot.co.uk.

Welsh Information Literacy blog,
    http://library.wales.org/informationliteracy/blog.

7

Developing students as readers

CILIP recommends that the librarian plays a lead role in developing a whole-school reading culture, promoting literacy and reading for pleasure. This means that:

- reading is seen as a whole-school issue and all subject departments appreciate their part in supporting wider reading
- the librarian makes a unique contribution to creating a reading culture through maintaining a good selection of appropriate resources and providing a wide range of promotional and developmental activities
- the librarian has a wide and up-to-date knowledge of young people's literature and uses this to support the individual needs of each member of the school community.

Introduction

The value of reading for pleasure has been recognized in recent reports from Ofsted (2012, 2013b) and the Department for Education (2012). That teachers themselves also appreciate the importance of reading, even when so many other pressures are upon them, is demonstrated by the National Union of Teachers (c.2010), which wrote: 'The active encouragement of reading for pleasure should be a core part of every child's educational entitlement, whatever their background or attainment, as extensive reading and exposure to a wide range of texts make a huge contribution to students' educational achievement.' Current research into young people's reading habits (Clark, 2012) reinforces the urgent need to identify innovative ways in which the relationship between the reader and the book can be explored, supported and stimulated, especially given the rapidly developing media and technological innovations competing for young people's time and attention.

School librarians are uniquely placed to make a significant contribution to the encouragement of reading and the creation of a reading culture across the whole school community. A knowledgeable school librarian has the skills to match individual students to reading materials most suited to their interests by having:

- an up-to-date and comprehensive knowledge of the current library stock
- a wide knowledge of contemporary books and publishing trends obtained by extensive personal reading as well as accessing current reviews in newspapers, professional library journals, specialist magazines and blogs, and through involvement with professional library organizations and networks
- an insight into students' curricular and non-curricular interests across the whole school community
- an overview of individual students as they progress through the school, and the ability to build up a profile of their reading habits and interests
- opportunities to engage with students in both formal and informal situations, during lessons and outside structured time.

The school librarian needs strategies to suit readers, as well as potential readers, regardless of their age, gender, background or previous reading experience. These strategies include:

- enthusing individual readers
- supporting specific groups
- being a reading role model
- enlisting the support of colleagues, both teaching and support staff, in raising the reading profile across the curriculum
- getting the whole school reading
- involving the community in reading initiatives
- forming reading partnerships with outside agencies including public libraries.

Thinking about specific aims will enable the targeting of clearly differentiated client groups in line with the current library improvement plan and budget.

Creating a whole-school reading culture

A whole-school approach that makes evidence of reading for pleasure as visible throughout the school as possible sends a powerful message. The librarian should take every opportunity to raise reading in the consciousness of the community.

Sharing activities can generate a huge interest in reading. Some simple but effective options are listed below.

1 Word-of-mouth recommendations.
2 Buddy schemes – pairing students to choose, read and share books together. The most common pairings are post-16 students and reluctant younger readers, 11-year-olds with 10-year-olds to ease primary/secondary transition, less able 15-year-olds with 13-year-old students to boost confidence and reading stamina. Adequate training for the supporting student is essential.
3 Reading groups – meeting before, during or after school where everyone reads the same book or within the same genre or recommends a personal favourite. Groups can be made up of single or mixed year groups, boys or girls only or fans of a particular title, series or author.
4 Author visits, live reading events, poetry performances and storytelling sessions.
5 Visits by creative artists or residencies, for example graphic novelists.
6 Book debates.
7 Shadowing schemes that follow national or regional book awards. The most established of these are CILIP's Carnegie Medal, awarded to outstanding books for children and young people, and the Greenaway Medal for illustrated books for children (CILIP, 2012).
8 Make good use of online facilities and social media and make reading more 'sociable' and interactive.
9 Screen savers across the school network that promote books and library events.
10 'Top ten' displays.
11 Create a reading calendar using national promotions for specific months or times of the year as the basis for reading activities. This will ensure something for all sectors of the school community at different times and stages of their school career. World Book Day, National Poetry Day and many others have stylish and professionally produced

promotional material alongside freely downloadable resources, helping to keep the profile of reading high all year round.

Harnessing young people's interest in mobile phones, videos, e-mail, computer gaming and the internet can be a powerful motivator for encouraging the regular reading habit. Content should, of course, always be checked before promoting sites, creating bookmarks and using online discussion groups. Policies should be compatible with all other school acceptable use policies and should be drawn up in consultation with users. Successful activities can include:

- text messaging or tweet reviews
- video book ads – staff talking about their favourite reads
- videoconferencing with other school reading groups
- videoconferencing an author visit
- creating snappy book/magazine jingles and trailers
- creating digital photograph displays
- devising a photostory
- developing a reading website
- participating in online reading discussions
- posting reviews
- creating bookmarks
- playing book-related online games
- taking part in virtual reading groups and festivals
- e-mailing authors.

Reading across the curriculum

Reading is no longer the preserve of the English department. As reading champion, the school librarian should take every opportunity to promote reading in every subject area, perhaps taking topic-linked boxes into classrooms, using fiction in tutorial and guidance lessons, picture books in child development, science fiction in physics or multicultural fiction in geography. The librarian should work with teachers to support reading around their subject for wider interest by, for example, creating subject-linked reading lists. Indeed, showing teachers the power of teacher recommendations to students and helping them to do this through display and library visits is an important role for the librarian.

The brain, learning and reading

Reading engages both emotion and intellect – left and right brain hemispheres – and thinking skills are very similar to what school librarians have traditionally taught as 'information-handling skills'. Keeping up to date with, understanding and adapting the latest theories will ensure that librarians are accepted as co-professionals in the educational arena. Useful references include:

- Claxton's learning dispositions (Claxton, 2000)
- Costa's habits of mind (Costa, 2000)
- Gardner's multiple intelligences (Gardner, 1985)
- Goleman's emotional intelligence (Goleman, 1996, 1999)
- Greenfield's brain research (Greenfield, 2000)
- Prashnig's learning styles (Prashnig, 1998).

For many students the electronic screen can provide a new way into books, whether by giving a different experience of reading or, on a practical level, allowing font sizes to be altered. Appropriate models for library delivery are still very much in flux, and school librarians will need to research the new models being offered and decide which is most appropriate for their needs.

Reading and the wider educational agenda

The school librarian should argue that putting reading at the centre of what the school does will positively enhance the school's aims and priorities in line with current educational agendas, such as:

- national priorities and initiatives
- citizenship
- peer mentoring
- social inclusion and disaffection
- equal opportunities
- lifelong learning
- personal and social development
- consultation with and involvement of students
- community partnerships
- the pastoral context and holistic development
- school self-evaluation processes.

Working with the individual

To really generate excitement around reading, librarians need to start with the young people themselves. Working in partnership with students in selecting (including visiting bookshops with them), displaying and promoting stock, changing displays, creating websites and organizing live reading events is vital to success. Such involvement carries implications for behaviour in the library, creates positive attitudes to reading and fulfils the active citizenship agenda. Above all, it is when working with the individual, using their knowledge of contemporary fiction to find each pupil books that he or she will enjoy, that librarians can be most effective.

Self-evaluation (see also Chapter 9)

The process of self-evaluation will address the following questions:

- How well does the librarian support the literacy objectives of the school?
- How well does the librarian promote reading for pleasure as an activity to be continued beyond school hours?
- How well do the library staff encourage students and staff to read widely and confidently?
- How well does the librarian develop the reading interests and abilities of all?

Evaluating and demonstrating the value-added impact of reading-related activities is crucial. Librarians should keep records of events and activities – library lesson bookings, overheard comments and anecdotes, increasing issue figures as a result of particular promotions or book events, reading diaries, photos, videos, individual success stories, teacher/parent comments, reader satisfaction surveys – and ensure that they are included in annual reports, school and local newspapers and staff meeting agendas.

These key questions are important in ensuring that the stock contains a wide range of reading opportunities with a good variety of genres and formats at different levels that offer both challenge and progression. The library services should validate all reading choices and both fiction and information books should be actively promoted. The old adage of 'the right book for the right reader at the right time' is never more true than during the secondary school years.

Useful websites

http://booksforkeeps.co.uk
www.booktrust.org.uk
www.fantasticfiction.co.uk
www.literacytrust.org.uk
www.lovereading.co.uk
www.readingagency.org.uk
www.teenreads.com

8

Marketing, promotion and advocacy

CILIP recommends that the librarian is proactive in marketing and promoting services, resources and library use. This means that:

- the librarian regularly gathers information on users' needs and compares these with service provision
- the librarian actively encourages use of the library and its resources
- the librarian champions the role of the library in supporting teaching and learning.

Introduction

'Marketing' is frequently associated with promotional activities and advertising but, in reality, it is a much broader management process which includes identifying, anticipating and satisfying customer requirements (Chartered Institute of Marketing, 2000). Librarians must continually ensure that their service is relevant to the needs of the school community and that it is promoted effectively to appropriate audiences and stakeholders, both existing and new. Using a marketing approach enables the librarian to be both genuinely responsive to needs and capable of anticipating and satisfying future requirements.

The marketing mix

There are key factors that determine users' perceptions of a service and that can be controlled to manage demand. These are referred to as the 'marketing mix' and are the basic considerations of any marketing strategy. A school librarian must honestly consider each of these in relation to the needs of all potential users to successfully market the library or a particular project. The '7 Ps' of marketing (Chartered Institute of Marketing, 2000) are:

1 **Product.** The range, quality and features of the services offered, including activities such as study support and reading groups, and the extent to which these reflect the needs of users and non-users.
2 **Price.** While the school library may be free at the point of access, there may be costs associated with its use which determine demand. For example, fines and charges for lost or damaged items can be a powerful deterrent to some users. On the other hand, sharing the costs of specific resources, such as online periodicals, with individual departments can have the effect of making them value the resource and be more determined to increase its use.
3 **Promotion.** Communication with all potential users through use of the school website, intranet, VLE, magazines, podcasts, presentations in assembly or to staff, governors' or management meetings. Different audiences require different styles of communication and different messages.
4 **Place/physical distribution.** Opening times, location of the library sites and opportunities for virtual access to resources from home or on mobile devices all have an impact on library use.
5 **People.** The knowledge, approach and accessibility of all library staff (school librarian and assistants along with any volunteers) are central to the library users' experience of the school library. Working out role rights with teaching colleagues is equally important. Some librarians develop a customer service charter to set expectations and standards of service.
6 **Process.** Users' experience of the library is enhanced when they find what they want quickly and easily. Signage, author or subject displays, reading trails and online learning activities, and podcasts that demonstrate a skill or task are some of the ways that librarians help their users.
7 **Physical evidence.** The building and design, layout and furnishings and ambience of the library will determine how attractive it is to potential users. Any online home pages will need to be equally attractive and accessible.

SWOT analysis

Before developing a marketing plan, it is helpful to reflect upon current practice by looking at the **S**trengths and **W**eaknesses, and the **O**pportunities for and **T**hreats to development. This is a SWOT analysis. The more users can be involved in this exercise, the better. This can be done with a series of small groups chosen to reflect the range of users and stakeholders. A brain-storming technique may help to identify the key strengths, weaknesses, opportunities and threats, and these can be recorded as shown in the example in Figure 8.1.

Strengths	Weaknesses
• Line manager is a senior leader and is very supportive • Fiction stock is up to date and in good condition • Many students have a positive attitude to reading • The library environment is attractive • The school library service loans support weak stock areas • An effective induction programme is in place	• Not enough easy chairs • Some very poor non-fiction stock (geography, maths, science) • English/Humanities block is a long way from the library • Not enough staff to supervise at lunchtimes • Insufficient money to replace 10% of stock annually • Information literacy skills embedded only in some curriculum areas • Lack of time to liaise with teachers
Opportunities	**Threats**
• Special measures status might bring opportunities to bid for money • A new subject head provides an opportunity to redefine the relationship between the library and that subject • The school wishes to raise the profile of reading for pleasure • A new web page manager is appointed • The English department is willing to allow Year 7 induction to take place in English lessons	• Special measures status might divert funds away from the library • Whole-school budget cuts • English department keen to purchase own resources, as library stock is poor • New VLE is unable to link to library catalogue • ICT support staff do not understand library needs and role

Figure 8.1 SWOT analysis example

Writing a marketing plan

Following the SWOT analysis, the marketing plan is drawn up. It will set out how a school library project will be developed, managed and promoted in response to the needs identified and will inform and be informed by the improvement plan. It will have four strands:

1 Needs analysis.
2 Demand forecasting and management.
3 Costing and resource management.
4 Promotion management.

Needs analysis

Profiling the needs of the school community is the first step in writing the school library policy or improvement plan, as well as in writing a marketing plan. Promotion is in itself useless unless the library has based its service on identified needs. It presents an opportunity for the school librarian to engage with the diversity of cultures, personal and social needs present within the school.

The data sources which can be used to determine the needs of the individual and general levels of demand are:

- surveys of student and staff attitudes to gauge users' and non-users' views and needs
- evidence from meetings, plans for school improvement or statements from staff about the projected demands that the curriculum and learning strategies will make on the library
- quantitative data gathered from the library management system or online resources giving information on patterns of use which can be analysed by, for example, gender or year groups
- comments from staff and student discussion groups
- feedback books, comment cards or Post-it notes for responses to library provision or suggestions for stock and services
- responses from user satisfaction questionnaires
- analysis of cultural diversity, including languages spoken within the home, and the range of faiths represented within the school
- socio-economic indicators, such as free school meals
- data on students with special educational needs or those identified as gifted and talented
- academic research profiling young people's attitudes to reading, learning, books, technology and information (e.g. Clark, 2012).

Demand forecasting and management

It is important to forecast the demand for a library service or project. The needs analysis will have revealed potential target groups for marketing. However, the demand from this market will be determined by other factors listed in the marketing mix. For example, what alternative activities are available in the school at the same time? How accessible and attractive is the library environment? What promotion will be undertaken to encourage use? How many students have adequate online access outside school? The school library is a place for the whole school community; however, the librarian may want to limit access at particular times to focus support on specific user groups in order to manage demand.

Costing and resource management

Allocating budget and time is part of the decision-making process and will be included in the library improvement plan. Factors may include:

- design and production of publicity materials
- fees for author visits and other activities involving external resources
- additional copies of books required for reading promotions
- staff time required for organization and implementation.

Guidance on the generation of a improvement plan and a budget is given in Chapters 2 and 3.

Promotion management

Promotion management is an important and highly visible component of marketing and has the definite aim of increasing use. However, library promotion sometimes stops short of this by increasing awareness but failing to actually impact on levels of use or deliver new users.

It is helpful to consider another marketing mnemonic: AIDA. This stands for Awareness, Interest, Desire and Action. This is a reminder that action will only happen if the first three have been achieved. First comes customer **awareness** of a service or opportunity, leading to an **interest** on their part. Then follows a **desire** to obtain the service or opportunity for themselves before **action** will take place. Action simply will not happen without the customer first being aware of, then interested in, and finally desirous of the particular product or service. In terms of library promotion, this means working at all three stages before an increase in use can be expected. An example might be:

Objective: to increase use of the library for homework after school.

Awareness: posters and leaflets advertising the opening hours and facilities are displayed and other methods of reaching students, such as announcements in assemblies, could be used as well.

Interest: the publicity messages include something to interest the students. Key phrases such as 'improve your homework marks' or 'somewhere to relax and do homework after school' or special attractions such as refreshments or the availability of extra help are highlighted to attract the target audience.

Desire: students see their peers enjoying visiting the library after school and more of them want to join in.

Action: if all these are successful, action (i.e. students attending) should follow. Once the programme has been implemented, it is important to measure the outcomes to see if the objectives were achieved.

Consideration may be given to library branding. A logo, a theme tune for videos or a colour scheme and in-house style for library publications help make it obvious to everyone that it is the library that is promoting and delivering the service or resource.

Methods of promotion

It is important to employ a variety of promotional methods. Over-exposure to even the best promotion can diminish its impact. Some, such as library displays, can be used throughout the school year and become a constant feature of library life. Others, owing to the time and resources needed to run them effectively, may be one-off or annual events only. It is useful to keep in mind the methods used by bookshops and other retail outlets frequented by young people in promoting their stock. In a bookshop every aspect of space and display is carefully designed to encourage the user to interact with the books. Shelving is not used just to store stock but also to promote it. Monitoring how users move around the library may lead to something like a pile of books being left out where students can browse through them; a simple idea that may have a big impact. Similarly, technology and social networking may be exploited to reach users beyond the library and draw them in. Using the VLE, for example, to create active links between subjects and the library may attract students to use the library by highlighting resources relevant to their current needs.

In the same way as a business analyses its customer relations, the librarian should think about its different groups of clientele and the ways in which the library can meet their needs. Some practical examples are given below.

Promotion to students

1 All new students are given a basic introduction to library facilities and services. This is reinforced whenever the curriculum demands the use of particular facilities or resources. Inductions are lively and interesting, presenting the library as 'user-friendly', and may include online tutorials or videos enabling users to access them when they need to.
2 Wider reading is promoted, as described in Chapter 7.
3 Staff are approachable and available to help students when they need it.

Promotion to governors and senior leaders

1 Regular reports to governors or the appointment of a link governor for the library help some librarians to sustain contacts with the school governors.
2 Reporting to senior leaders via the line management and performance management structures (as outlined in Chapter 2) ensures a line of communication between the librarian and senior leaders.

Promotion to teaching staff

Different avenues for promoting the library to teachers are:

Leadership

1 The library improvement plan reflects the whole-school plan and relevant features of department plans and drive discussions accordingly.

2 The use of the library is an item to be addressed as part of every department's self-evaluation.
3 The librarian attends relevant meetings including whole-staff, departmental, heads of departments, working parties, and curriculum development.

Interpersonal

The involvement of the librarian in other school activities and being seen in the staff room during breaks and lunchtimes are invaluable in giving unexpected opportunities for informal promotion at the point of need.

Communication

1 Consulting staff, whether formally via surveys or informally, to seek their views about the library resources and services, is a good way to open up dialogue and build relationships.
2 The librarian makes use of whatever staff newsletters, briefings or staff meetings exist within the school to give out news of library activities. Staff e-mail or the VLE may be used to maintain staff awareness of new stock, services and activities.
3 Selective dissemination of information that saves teachers time and stress will demonstrate the value of the library service. Maintaining a file of individual teachers' specific interests and requirements will help the librarian to target this work.

INSET

1 Induction sessions for new staff and student teachers, including a tour of the library where resources specific to their curriculum area and interests can be promoted, give the librarian the opportunity to make an impression at a time when people are often open to new ideas and eager to collaborate.
2 INSET days held within the library and concentrating on library issues can be of enormous benefit in raising the profile of the library and showing how it can help teachers in the delivery of the curriculum. The local school library service, if available, should be able to help with

planning and delivering a very effective day's or half-day's training, aimed at the whole staff or selected departments or year groups.

Promotion to parents and the wider community

Librarians should ensure that parents receive positive messages about the library early on in their child's life at the school. It is unhelpful if the only communication they receive from the library is an overdue notice. Some ideas are listed below:

1 Parent evenings for parents and carers to browse library resources, including ICT equipment and digital resources, and to see examples of work undertaken in the library.
2 Open days in the library, when parents, governors, students and the wider community can visit and students are on hand to act as guides.
3 Curriculum evenings, when the librarian can host activities or run a session on the role of the library in students' learning.
4 Parent–teacher association (PTA) liaison to ensure members are fully aware of the role of the library as a particularly cost-effective means of managing resources.
5 Communication with parents, either via a library newsletter or newspaper or through regular contributions from the library to the school's own newsletter to parents. Facilities such as text messaging to parents and parent portals may also be available.
6 Reports about library activities in the local media and on the school website.
7 Volunteers in schools – individuals often volunteer to help in schools, including in the library and with reading programmes. Their help can be very welcome and strengthens links between the school, parents and the local community. This should always be arranged in accordance with the school's safeguarding procedures.

Advocacy

Advocacy is speaking out and winning influence. As education policy tends towards the delegation of management responsibility to each school it is increasingly important for librarians to act as advocates within their own schools. Usual targets will be the senior leadership team, governors, the parents and the teaching staff. Advocacy can assist the school librarian in gaining:

- improved status amongst conflicting and competing priorities
- funding from limited budgets
- new partners who appreciate the library's importance
- recognition of the library's activities as central to the school's mission from head teachers and governors.

Advocacy requires a combination of strategies, with a clear identification of:

- the target audience to be influenced, which may be any one of those mentioned above
- the identification of the advocacy message by deciding precisely what the target audience needs to know, being as concise and economical as possible
- the strategy for getting the advocacy message to the target audience, including many of the methods outlined in the above section on promotion
- the evidence – national and international research is powerful (see online resources detailed below); so too is evidence collected from evaluation of outcomes on learning and teaching in the school (see Chapter 9).

An example of a tool which employs these strategies is SLG's own leaflet (School Libraries Group, 2013), which is aimed at helping parents and governors to ask questions about school libraries they visit. It has a clear target audience, a specific need identified and uses key quotes from research.

Online advocacy resources

CILIP, www.cilip.org.uk/cilip/advocacy-awards-and-projects/advocacy-and-campaigns/school-libraries.

International Association of School Librarianship, www.iasl-online.org/advocacy/make-a-difference.html.

School Library Association, www.sla.org.uk/advocacy-and-promotion.php.

9

Evaluation

CILIP recommends that the librarian regularly evaluates the performance of the library. This means that:

- the librarian is fully integrated into the school's annual planning and improvement cycle
- evidence of the impact and outcomes of the librarian's work is collected
- the librarian has a vehicle for dialogue with stakeholders throughout the whole school community
- the librarian has a body of evidence underpinning his/her professional status.

Introduction

Evaluation is a key part of a school's cycle of planning and development and the evaluation of the library is an important element in that process. This chapter will cover:

- the management of evaluation
- types of evidence to be gathered
- the difference between inputs, outputs and outcomes
- the main approaches to evaluation
- using the results of evaluation
- the benefits of evaluation.

Evaluation provides valuable evidence of good practice. It can and should inform target setting and strategic planning. Figure 9.1 on the next page illustrates this point.

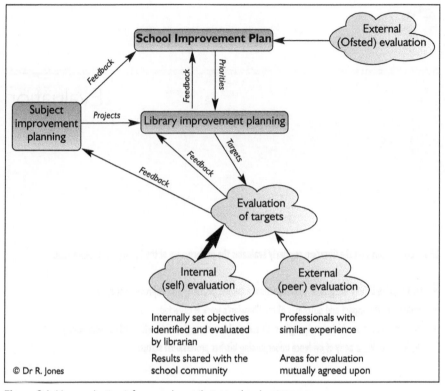

Figure 9.1 How evaluation informs and contributes to the planning process

Service evaluation should determine the library's improvement plans. Self-evaluation informs the professional development agenda of the librarian. These are related but discrete activities; service evaluation may inform self-evaluation but is not the sole determining factor. It is powerful advocacy evidence for making a case for new services, resources, staffing or infrastructure.

Effective management is only possible with effective evaluation. It is how the school librarian can evidence outcomes. There is a growing emphasis on self-evaluation and it is a trend that the librarian should welcome. It provides a timely opportunity to be part of the wider agenda and to claim a central and vital role in the life of the school as one of its key stakeholders.

Evaluating the library requires progress to be measured against agreed priorities and objectives using a variety of techniques. These involve monitoring, collecting data to measure performance, evaluating performance through performance indicators, reporting on progress and reviewing targets and objectives. The cycle is shown in Figure 9.2.

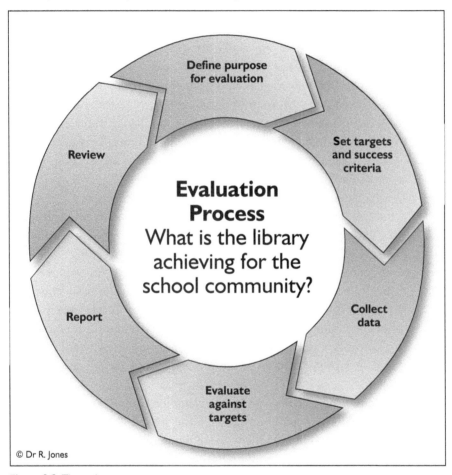

© Dr R. Jones

Figure 9.2 The evaluation process

The evaluation process

1 **Monitoring** is the ongoing process of collecting and analysing data. Data should include quantitative data (i.e. numeric measures) and qualitative data (i.e. descriptive evidence of what is happening). The best way of gathering qualitative data is through consultations, interviews, surveys and observations.

2 **Performance measures** show what is happening or has happened. These might include book issues by gender and year group or from a specific section of the library. They are useful for building performance indicators.

3 **Performance indicators** enable evaluation through the use of comparisons. Comparisons are made with the library's past performance (e.g. last term or last year), or with other comparable libraries or services (benchmarking). They can be quantitative or qualitative:

- *Quantitative performance indicators* at their best combine two data sets from at least two performance measures to give useful indicators of the levels of actual performance, such as the change in fiction loans to girls following an author visit. The school librarian's challenge is to select the most appropriate indicators to use to reflect progress towards the library's main objectives or targets.

- *Qualitative performance indicators* describe a target level of achievement. For example, 'The library is perceived by senior leaders to be at the heart of the school' or 'The library encourages reading for pleasure and develops individual students in their reading confidence'. Objective evidence for these indicators can be more difficult to obtain. The evidence might come from staff and student surveys or interviews, the degree of attention the library gets in key school documents, or from observations and evidence from parents or governors. Qualitative evidence has much greater currency than might be expected; it is an important vehicle for student and staff voice.

4 **Reporting on progress.** The results of evaluation should be used to report to others on the role the library plays in the school. Regular appropriate reporting will alert others to the work of the library, and the contribution it makes to learning and teaching. This can be done in an annual report or through special reports or bids for funding.

5 **Reviewing targets and objectives.** Once a year, the library's key objectives and targets should be reviewed as part of the improvement planning process. At the same time, performance measures and indicators should be reviewed. New performance indicators will need to be developed for any new priority areas, and can be used in the improvement plan to show how progress towards the targets will be measured.

Data collection
Inputs

Inputs are traditionally the type of evaluation data most frequently used by librarians. They describe the resources, investment and time that go into the library service. These inputs can be considered against benchmarks (e.g. measures of what the best school libraries are achieving) or against recommendations (e.g. from CILIP, DfE, HMI or the SLA). School library services can advise about local, national or regional benchmarks. The input *measures* that should be monitored and recorded include:

- what space the library occupies against recommended levels (see Chapter 4)
- whether the library is staffed by an appropriately qualified librarian with head of department status
- the total annual stock budget
- whether the range of stock reflects all National Curriculum and literacy requirements, and all age and ability levels
- the library's opening hours and the extent to which they allow access to both class groups and individual users.

Input *performance indicators* will include:

- the total/average per student expenditure on the library and resources compared to recommended levels (see Chapter 5)
- the percentage of the stock and resources that fully reflect issues of diversity and special needs and are genuinely inclusive
- the level of good-quality stock per student against the recommended levels of 13 per student for 11–16 schools and 17 for 16–18 schools.

Input data is usually the easiest to capture and analyse. It neither describes what use is made of the library service, nor what the impact is on students, teachers and the wider community. It is important therefore that it is combined with and used alongside measures of outputs and, most significantly, of outcomes.

Outputs

Outputs describe the level and frequency of activity. They can be calculated through the use of electronic gate counts or computer management systems. They can be evaluated against targets (for instance, an increase of $x\%$ in items loaned annually), or against benchmarks (e.g. the output levels that the best school libraries are achieving). Output *measures* that may be monitored include:

- the number of items loaned
- the number of enquiries
- the number of class visits to the library
- the number of individual library users
- the number of literacy-related activities in the library
- the number of and attendance at other reading development activities, reading promotions, etc.
- the frequency of and attendance at out-of-school-hours activities
- the number of students undertaking programmes of library skills induction and development in each separate year group
- the number of students displaying competence at using the skills they have been taught.

Output *performance indicators* might include:

- the percentage of membership (staff and students) using the library/borrowing items
- the percentage of classes making systematic use of the library
- the percentage of students attending out-of-school-hours activities
- the percentage of students who display competence in using the library skills they have been taught.

Specific outputs can also be used to learn the extent to which the library is engaging with particular target groups:

- loans by year groups
- loans by gender
- loans by specific, target groups (e.g. special educational needs, free school meals or white British boys)
- use of the library by particular departments.

Outputs alone have a limited power as evaluation data, as they do not indicate whether the activity is actually achieving any impact on users. At best, outputs can demonstrate user awareness, activity and satisfaction.

Outcomes or impacts

Outcomes or impacts describe the *effect* of the service's inputs and outputs. They can be used to show how people develop, learn and change as a result of the services of the librarian. They can show the difference that the school librarian makes to individuals, groups and the whole school community. Outcomes are the most powerful evaluation data that the school librarian can use. However, they can be the hardest to measure.

Outcomes can encompass a whole range of behavioural changes. They might demonstrate that students are more motivated and engaged, or that they are reading in new and exciting ways. They might demonstrate that teachers are using new resource-based teaching strategies as a result of the school librarian's work. They might describe the way students behave as independent learners in the library, both in lesson times and outside them. They might provide evidence of changes in attitude, motivation or level of study skills. These outcomes provide the evidence that the librarian has had an impact.

Outcomes are usually gathered through qualitative data. To evaluate an outcome it is necessary to go through three stages:

1 Select an appropriate outcome that reflects a school priority or a particular chosen focus (e.g. 'more children will enjoy reading for pleasure').
2 Consider what the success criteria are for that outcome, that is, which signs will show that the outcome is occurring and a positive impact is taking place (e.g. more children will express enjoyment in discussing their reading; teachers will report more children enjoying reading for pleasure).
3 Decide how to collect the evidence to show that this is happening (e.g. How many children borrow books for pleasure and express enjoyment about them? What do teachers say?)

Outcome evidence that can be collected includes:

- examples of students' talking or writing about what they have enjoyed or learnt through the library
- examples from teachers and parents, showing how students' learning has been supported by the library
- observation of students' behaviour in the library relating to library intervention; this might include a wider reading range or improved information retrieval skills.

Inspiring Learning (MLA, 2008) contains planning and assessment tools for librarians to use to review, measure and improve performance of their services.

Consultation with students and staff

Consultation is a key way of collecting evidence for evaluation. Evidence drawn from the users of the library, and from the non-users, will be key to evaluating the extent to which the library impacts upon the school. The question 'How can students and teachers help to provide the evidence?' should be asked and answered in every evaluation exercise.

Approaches to evaluation

There are three main approaches to evaluation. These are self-evaluation, peer review and external evaluation.

Self-evaluation

Self-evaluation is the term used to describe the process in which the service is assessed against objectives by its own internal management. It demands a rigorous, open, honest and objective approach to assessing the value and effectiveness of the service involved. It has the advantage of being an in-house process, the control of which lies with the manager directly responsible for the service. A key strength of self-evaluation is that significant factors will not be overlooked through ignorance.

Increasingly, self-evaluation is being recognized as a key strategy for improving standards in schools. Inspection agencies are actively encouraging, and in some cases, requiring, self-evaluation. In response, models of self-evaluation were developed for school libraries. Streatfield and Markless (2004) and Scottish Library and Information Council (2009) are good examples of these.

To be effective, self-evaluation needs to be as objective as possible and maintain a clear focus on outcomes rather than on processes. It requires a basic project plan and a specific timescale. The findings and conclusions from self-evaluation should be used as a basis of revising the school improvement plan.

In planning self-evaluation, the following key points need to be considered:

Which area of the service to evaluate

It is unlikely that self-evaluation will examine all areas of the library service. It is much more likely that a specific area will be addressed initially and over a period of time the self-evaluation process can gradually cover all key areas of the library service. The focus of the self-evaluation needs to be selected by the school librarian and is a good vehicle with which to align the library services to the school improvement plan. Consideration may also be given to any areas that are currently on the political and national education agenda and which fall under the remit of the school librarian, by consulting relevant documentation from Ofsted or the Department for Education.

Support for self-evaluation

The support of the school's senior leadership for self-evaluation is key for winning support for any resulting action plans. An external 'critical friend' may also help by providing an objective perspective during the self-evaluation process. This role could be undertaken by a senior professional library colleague from another school or the local school library service.

What data to collect and how to collect it

Tools that can be used to collect data for electronic questionnaires include Survey Monkey (www. surveymonkey.com). Factors such as acceptable response rate, potential bias and anonymity should be considered. Soliciting the opinions of the students can be a very powerful tool. However, it is important to understand they will answer within the limits of their existing knowledge and understanding. For example, asking how many students would like to see PlayStation games loaned in the library will get a better response than asking students what new services they would like the library to provide, as trying to imagine new services that are outside their experience is challenging for anyone. It is important to understand that with any survey the results will be heavily influenced by the questions asked. Care should be taken to avoid an undesired outcome through badly designed questions – for example, polling for a service which the librarian is unlikely to be able to deliver.

Drawing conclusions and sharing them

The evidence should be collated and then analysed for key messages about the impact the library is having. The librarian will then produce a summary of findings and draw some conclusions and recommendations in the light of what has been learned. For example, if the impact study shows that in relation to independent learning the library is felt to have a significant impact on student skills for a particular year group, it may be appropriate to recommend extending the information-skills programme to other years. The findings will be a powerful lever to support library development. They need also to be presented to the wider school community, especially to the senior leadership team and to governors.

Peer review

Peer review is a valuable form of evaluation, which combines the rigour of external inspection with the informed view of the specialist. Peer review takes place where one or more professionals with a similar background and experience, but who work in an external context, provide external evaluation combined with ideas and support. It can be a reciprocal arrangement, where staff from different schools can agree to review one another's performance.

Peer review can be useful for comparing outputs and for evaluating outcomes. It can be used to compare data, or it can be used to evaluate how things are done and whether there are alternative ways of achieving the same or improved outcomes. The results of peer review can be used in exactly the same way as those from self-evaluation.

External evaluation

Schools are systematically appraised by statutory inspections, which are performed by Ofsted and ISI, government approved inspectorates. It would be natural to expect these bodies to evaluate the school library and highlight its impact on learning and teaching. However, in practice, many inspections fail to engage rigorously with the school library. It is therefore the responsibility of the librarian, with the necessary support and recognition of their senior leadership team, to ensure that the library's planning and evaluation is part of, and indeed embedded in, the school's own self-evaluation form (SEF) and improvement planning cycle. It will then be expected that the confirmation of the library's contribution to the school, through these documents, will form important evidence for management to present to inspectors, as it will be a necessary part of the school's planning and evaluation. In order to do this, the librarian must be part of the improvement planning cycle, as discussed in Chapter 3. Ofsted (2013a) states that 'Self-evaluation provides the basis for planning, development and improvement in schools', which is why it is so important to be part of this necessary and powerful procedure.

Recent reports from Ofsted will be particularly pertinent starting points for a librarian's improvement planning. For example, 'Moving English Forward' (Ofsted, 2012) advocates a greater emphasis on reading for pleasure within the taught curriculum in both primary and secondary schools. It goes on to say that 'Inspection evidence suggests that it is now time to take more practical steps to improve provision for reading in schools . . . working with the school librarian, and advising teachers in other subject areas how they might encourage reading for pleasure across the curriculum' (Ofsted, 2012, 43–4). This, therefore, highlights the importance the Government places on reading. They stress expectations that schools should be developing students' appreciation of literature. Ofsted expects to find evidence of students reading for pleasure. By having an awareness of these current and potential future developments and points of inspection, librarians can tailor their improvement planning to meet these priorities.

In order to gain the most benefit from any inspection, it is essential that the school librarian should prepare thoroughly. Evidence should be prepared and gathered in an accessible format ready to share with the external inspectors. It is always advisable to assume that the inspectors will have limited knowledge and understanding of the school library and so it is important not to omit information that may seem obvious to the school librarian. Preparation might include a portfolio of evidence forwarded to the inspection team in advance including:

- self-evaluation of the school library
- evidence of impact and outcomes on teaching, learning, reading and engagement
- evidence of out-of-school-hours activities
- a summary of quantitative data showing the level of basic library activity in terms of inputs and outputs, such as an annual report.

The value of external inspection is that the school library is measured alongside all other aspects of the school. Where the inspection identifies the value of the library to the quality of teaching and learning, this can be a powerful support for future school library development.

Using the results of evaluation

Evaluation is not a standalone activity but needs to be linked into a cycle of continuous improvement and development. The results should be used to inform the librarian's plans, policies and practice. They should be shared widely within the school to enable library development to be closely linked to whole-school developments. Difficult messages from the evidence should not be ignored but need to be confronted and reported to management as appropriate. The findings can be used in a variety of ways, such as:

- New priorities and plans may be identified for the improvement plan.
- Evidence may be used to secure funding for development.
- Budget priorities may shift.
- The arrangement of stock may be changed to improve accessibility.
- New promotions may be arranged to develop awareness of some services or resources.
- New ideas may be piloted to achieve specific aims.
- Simple operational changes might be made in the way the library operates for students and teachers.
- The results of evaluation, and especially any changes in policy and practice that are made as a result, should be published and made available.

The benefits of evaluation

Evaluation should be used to track progress towards the library's aims and results used to show progress against key areas of the library policy and the improvement plan. It should also, most importantly, include the ways in which students are using and benefiting from library resources and services. In other words, it should demonstrate what the library is achieving for the school community. A significant question for the school librarian should be 'To what extent is the library an asset to the school, and can it demonstrate that it makes a difference to learning and teaching?' An effective school librarian needs this information in order to plan for continuous improvement of the library and its services. Evaluation skills are therefore central to a good librarian's portfolio of skills.

The benefits of evaluation

10

Partnerships

CILIP recommends that the librarian works with key internal and external partners to improve the quality of the school library. This means that:

- the librarian accesses a range of external providers when necessary to supplement the school library provision and advises users accordingly
- the librarian uses all available sources of professional support to maintain current awareness and gain advice and training
- the librarian builds relationships with librarians and other professions to exchange ideas and collaborate on developments
- the librarian builds relationships with the local and wider community for the benefit of students
- the school provides the means and support for the librarian to sustain these contacts.

Introduction

As schools are increasingly seen within the context of the wider education community, the need for the school librarian to be at the hub of a network of learning partnerships is more important than ever before. The school librarian will develop and manage a range of partners. These will be determined by the school's aims, as reflected in the library improvement plan, and can offer significant benefits to each partner, including:

- achievement of plans, objectives and targets
- mutual support
- sharing of resources and activities leading to value for money

- joint planning and shared activities leading to good use of time
- learning from others and sharing experiences, saving valuable time
- sponsorship
- raised profile of the library and the school.

Internal partnerships

Internal partnerships may be developed with:

- senior leaders
- pastoral leaders
- curriculum leaders
- organizers of school clubs and societies
- enrichment and Gifted and Talented co-ordinators
- learning support staff
- careers advisers
- transition co-ordinators
- literacy and numeracy co-ordinators
- English as an additional language co-ordinator
- the safeguarding team
- student councils.

External partnerships

External partnerships may be developed with:

- school library services
- public libraries
- the wider school community
- parents
- feeder schools
- further and higher learning institutions
- other local authority services (youth services, social care services)
- the book trade
- national organizations
- international organizations.

School library services (SLSs)

School library services are run by local authorities. The School Library Association (www.sla.org.uk) and the Association of Senior Children's and Education Librarians (www.ascel.org.uk) maintain current lists of all SLSs. In authorities where they do not exist, schools may be able to buy into the services of neighbouring authorities. There is considerable variation in the way services operate. Often schools subscribe to their local school library service on behalf of all their teachers but some authorities pay for the service from central funds, so it is free at the point of delivery to schools.

According to the National Literacy Trust (2010), SLSs can give good value for money and are a cost-effective way of providing, among many other things, current and reliable loan resources when needed to meet specific and specialized demand. However, although they are often regarded primarily as the supplier of physical resources, it is the information management expertise of their experienced and qualified librarians and awareness of government priorities and policies relating to literacy and learning which can be a powerful force in supporting schools in delivering national and local strategies. In addition, some SLSs organize or co-ordinate specific projects or programmes, such as book awards, which are instrumental in building positive co-operation and cohesion between schools and within communities.

Services offered by school library services

Each SLS will provide full details of the support and services offered, and where applicable, the cost of this support. The services to schools will either be in the form of a pick-and-mix menu, a predefined package of services or a mixture of both. These will generally include some, if not all, of the following elements:

- consultancy and practical help
- support for evaluation
- training
- learning resource provision
- partnership development and networking opportunities
- initiatives to support the encouragement of wider reading.

Consultancy and practical support

SLSs offer a wide range of consultancy services. They will know of examples of good practice in their areas. Most SLSs will advise on:

- strategies for partnership working within the school, e.g. with teaching departments and colleagues
- library policy, budgeting and improvement planning
- the development of whole-school information literacy strategies
- the implementation of new technologies
- reader development initiatives, either within the school or in partnership with other schools as part of national schemes
- the design, planning and equipping of new or refurbished school libraries
- the recruitment of school library staff
- day-to-day library management.

Some SLSs will help with practical tasks which may be difficult for the school librarian, working alone, to fit into a busy schedule. This might include help with stock editing, rearrangement of shelving following refurbishment or the annual stock check. This may incur some additional cost but is worth considering if it means that a time-consuming, routine task will be completed efficiently within a defined timescale.

Support for evaluation

SLSs can assist with:

- the preparation for and response to external inspection
- the implementation of action plans, particularly in areas such as improving the standards of the school library and in information literacy skills provision
- strategies and procedures for self-evaluation. SLS staff can act as a 'critical friend', supporting the school librarian in self-evaluating. The SLS may also be able to advise on or even organize opportunities for peer review
- benchmarking – some SLSs collate data relating to school library provision which enable schools to benchmark themselves against local, regional or national levels and trends.

Training

Most SLSs offer INSET for teachers and librarians. Training is available from a range of providers but the local SLS can often provide training based on specific requirements or circumstances affecting the local area.

Learning resource provision

SLSs lend large numbers of resources in a wide variety of formats. These are carefully selected to meet the needs of pupils of all ages and abilities and of the curriculum. SLSs also assist schools to select resources for purchase through book talks, bibliographies, electronic resources, exhibition collections and bookshop services. Some SLSs offer 'shelf-ready' stock from a book supplier, complete with classification, jacketing and other stationery. As well as non-book resources such as CDs, DVDs, audios and artefacts, some SLSs have established consortia for the purchase of online resources. Economies of scale, centralized co-ordination and technical support make this an attractive package for schools.

Partnership development and networking opportunities

The SLS is the focal point for school librarians within an area, facilitating networking and professional meetings where knowledge, experience and good practice can be shared. The SLS can act as an important bridging agency linking the school library with the local public library service and other local authority services and departments.

Reader development and reading for pleasure opportunities

SLSs are passionate about the importance of children reading for pleasure, and can support this through:

- loans of high-quality fiction and poetry which can be exchanged regularly
- loans of books to meet special requests, dual- and foreign-language books and large-print books
- provision of storysacks offering artefacts to extend the story
- support for the organization of reading groups and book award shadowing

- organization and delivery of book promotion events such as reading debates, poetry slams and author visits
- provision of book magazines and reading lists offering recommended reads
- advice to schools to help them to buy good-quality new books and in some cases offering a book purchase scheme offering good discounts
- training courses for teachers and school library staff
- help with the development of a school Reading for Pleasure policy.

Making best use of the SLS resources

The individual school will decide the nature and level of support to be requested from the SLS. One key decision is the balance to be made between resources that are purchased directly, and those borrowed or leased from the SLS. The decision should be informed by the considerations listed below.

Purchasing resources is the most appropriate decision for:

- items that are needed frequently
- items that are needed to form the core stock of the school library.

Hiring or leasing resources may be more appropriate for:

- items that are used only occasionally
- new items that the librarian wants to trial before purchase
- items where the library will benefit from a regular changeover of stock
- items needed for a short-term purpose; e.g. an exhibition or display on a particular topic, a topic being studied by a group of students for a particular time period, or extra books on a topic where there is considerable demand at one time.

Public libraries

Co-ordination of reader-development and study-support initiatives between the school library and local public library is useful and helps to avoid expensive and unnecessary duplication. If pupils are encouraged to register with their local public library they will gain access to online reference resources which can save the school a lot of money. Public and school libraries may also collaborate to promote family literacy and ensure that students are familiar and comfortable with using the public library, perhaps through a programme of class visits.

The wider school community

Parents

Chapter 8 discusses many ways of promoting the library to parents but building partnerships with parents is about more than just keeping them informed.

1 The home is a powerful influence on a young person and parents who are well informed about their child's reading can make a huge difference to their attitude to reading and learning. Guidance may be given at parents' meetings or through leaflets and booklists. Librarians can inform parents of achievements and concerns, with the appropriate measures to be taken, by using the school's established methods of praise and reporting. These may include parent/teacher consultation evenings and official school reports to parents.
2 Special projects involving parents might include library exhibitions or author visits, 'lads and dads' projects, special events or regular out-of-school clubs or homework sessions. Individuals often volunteer to help in schools, including in the library and with reading programmes. Their help can be very welcome and strengthens links between the school, parents and the local community. However, librarians must be aware of the Criminal Record Bureau barring procedures.

Feeder schools

Collaboration between primary schools and secondary school librarians can support the pupils' smooth transition between Key Stage 2 and Key Stage 3 education. Library provision in primary schools varies and some pupils may not have experienced any formal loans systems or classified collections of information resources. It is important that the secondary school librarian does not make false assumptions about the new intakes' ability to use the library confidently and effectively. A visit to the secondary school library can be a significant confidence booster for Year 6 pupils just before they move. Projects may include secondary students acting as reading mentors in primary schools or author events involving pupils from both primary and secondary schools.

Further and higher learning institutions

As with feeder school partnerships, closer links between the libraries in secondary schools, Sixth Form colleges and further education institutions help students to benefit from the services offered by all three. Initiatives include access to one another's catalogues and collections, joint staff training and co-ordinated approaches to developing information literacy.

Neighbouring secondary schools

Partnerships between neighbouring school librarians helps mitigate the professional isolation of solo practitioners. They can share expertise and plan joint events. Funding for specific areas of resource development may be shared and the costs for special events such as author visits can be borne jointly. School reading groups can use technologies such as Skype, video conferencing and social networking sites to hold virtual meetings, as long as the arrangements comply with school policy.

Other local authority services

Youth service

The school library is a unique and neutral location for the provision of resources to support individual and personal development, social information and career choices. Although the shape of youth services is changing dramatically within local authorities, there may be opportunities for successful partnership working particularly to encourage and support young people's participation and engagement in a local youth council or similar initiative.

Children's social care services

Social care services for children and young people within the local authority can provide valuable information on child protection issues and support for disabled children and children in care or at risk.

The book trade

To be effective, partnerships with publishers, local booksellers, authors, illustrators, poets, storytellers and performers need to be meaningful, with mutual benefits and each partner being aware of what they can contribute as well as what they can gain from it. Benefits for school libraries can include:

- support with planning and delivering a reading promotion
- access to authors, illustrators, poets, performers and storytellers who will come into school to deliver creative reading experiences
- provision of publicity and promotional materials for events and reading promotions
- improved current awareness with information on new books and pre-publication proof copies of books.

Benefits for book trade partners can include:

- feedback on pre-publication or newly published books
- raised awareness of new and debut authors
- increased book sales
- opportunities for an individual author to develop a relationship with readers at a local school
- successful author promotional tours
- raised awareness of local bookshops with local children and families who will be their target customers.

Most publishers, booksellers, book trade organizations and many authors, illustrators, poets, storytellers and performers have their own websites. In addition, there are review websites and websites that offer a portal into the world of children's books. The following are just a small selection of these:

www.authorsalouduk.co.uk
http://.booksforkeeps.co.uk
www.carnegiegreenaway.org.uk
www.carouselguide.co.uk
http://contactanauthor.co.uk
www.lovereading4kids.co.uk
www.mrsmad.com

www.readingzone.com
www.ukchildrensbooks.co.uk

National and international organizations

Developing national and international partnerships offers a rich range of opportunities to extend the horizons of the school and its community and build cultural capital and understanding. This section highlights some potential key partners:

Booktrust (www.booktrust.org.uk)

Booktrust is a reading and writing charity that administers a number of book gifting programmes and children's book prizes as well as offering advice and recommendations to readers and writers. These include:

- Children's Book Week – an annual celebration of reading for pleasure with activity ideas for celebrating reading for pleasure in schools
- Letterbox Club – focusing on improving the educational outlook for children aged 7–13 in foster families by providing them with a parcel of books, maths activities and educational materials every month for six months
- Bookbuzz – a reading programme from Booktrust targeting children aged 11, that supports schools to encourage reading for pleasure, independent choice and develop a whole school reading culture
- Beyond Booked Up – a programme aimed at pupils in both Year 7 and 8 that includes a range of accessible resources designed to help develop speaking, listening, writing and reading skills for 11–13-year-olds.

The Reading Agency (www.readingagency.org.uk)

The Reading Agency is a charity which runs creative programmes that help people feel inspired and confident about reading. They reach readers through UK-wide reading programmes, delivered in partnership with UK libraries, schools, prisons, workplaces, publishers and the media. Programmes include:

- Chatterbooks reading clubs – helping children build a lifelong reading habit. They are aimed at 4–14-year-olds, with clubs running all over the country in libraries, schools and wherever people want to set them up. Chatterbooks clubs are where children can have a really good time talking about books. Resources can be purchased to support the clubs and training courses are also available to help staff in setting up and running a club.

- The Six Book Challenge. One in six adults struggles to read. This programme improves the chances in life for people who find reading difficult, by building their reading confidence, motivation and literacy skills. The Six Book Challenge invites participants to pick six reads and record their reading in a diary in order to get a certificate.

National Literacy Trust (www.literacytrust.org.uk)

The National Literacy Trust is an independent charity that believes everyone in the UK should have the literacy skills they need. They work to improve reading, writing, speaking and listening skills through:

- sharing research, promoting best practice and providing support and resources
- campaigning to improve public understanding of the vital importance of literacy and to ensure the Government takes action.

They also provide a range of community literacy projects, which includes:

- National Literacy Network – supporting professionals who work in or with schools to raise literacy attainment, through practical support for the classroom and library, exciting CPD opportunities and a forum to learn from others in the network
- The Young Readers Programme – working in targeted locations to motivate disadvantaged children and young people to read for pleasure
- Premier League Reading Stars – a programme to harness the motivational power of football to encourage pupils to improve their literacy skills
- Words for Work – unlocking young people's speaking and listening skills for future employability.

Federation of Children's Book Groups (www.fcbg.org.uk)

The Federation of Children's Book Groups is a national voluntary self-funded organization whose aim is to promote enjoyment and interest in children's books and reading, to encourage the availability of books for children of all ages and to nurture a love of reading through the sharing of books with children. There are groups all around the UK and members include parents and carers, teachers and librarians. Activities include:

- the Red House Children's Book Award and Annual Award Ceremony
- local events for families and for schools focused around national initiatives such as National Share-A-Story Month, National Non-Fiction Day and other events such as World Book Day
- competitions, free gifts, books and resources designed for Federation members
- events for adults including author dinners, one-day conferences and attending the FCBG Annual Conference
- book swaps, book donations and reading groups
- *Carousel* magazine and a national newsletter.

International Federation of Library Associations and Institutions (IFLA, www.ifla.org/about)

IFLA is the leading international body representing the interests of library and information services and their users. It is the global voice of the library and information profession. It is an independent, non-governmental, not-for-profit organization that works through its 'sections'. Three sections which will be of particular interest for school librarians are:

1 **School Libraries and Resource Centres,** providing an international forum for exchanging ideas, experiences, research results and advocacy.
2 **Libraries for Children and Young Adults.** Two programmes that encourage partnership working have been developed by this section. The Sister Libraries Programme, which promotes the twinning of libraries, gives librarians the opportunity to exchange knowledge, information, resources, experience and ideas with colleagues in other countries. This opens up a range of new possibilities and can provide a channel for professional stimulation, motivation and dialogue and thus help

circumvent professional isolation and stagnation. It also gives young people the opportunity to increase their knowledge of another culture and their understanding of what other children enjoy reading. The World Through Picture Books programme lists picture books from around the world that have been recommended by librarians, as a tool for building bridges and developing understanding between countries. These lists can then be used as a way of celebrating and promoting the languages, cultures and quality of children's publishing around the world.

3 **Literacy and Reading** provides a focal point for the promotion of reading and literacy in libraries and the integration of reading research and reading development activities into library service. It seeks to raise social awareness of the significance of reading and general literacy.

Each section takes part in IFLA's World Library and Information Congress, which attracts over 3000 delegates from around the world and all sectors of librarianship. It provides school librarians with an opportunity to extend their own professional development and put librarianship and literacy into an international context.

International Association of School Librarianship (IASL, www.iasl-online.org/index.htm)

IASL provides an international forum for promoting school libraries. It holds an annual conference and promotes International School Library Month and International School Library Day. *School Libraries Worldwide* is published twice yearly and IASL also runs the GiggleIT Project, promoting creative writing.

International Board on Books for Young People (IBBY, www.ibby.org.uk)

IBBY is a non-profit organization with 70 national sections all over the world, including IBBY UK. It represents countries with well developed book publishing and literacy programmes, and other countries with only a few dedicated professionals who are doing pioneer work in children's book publishing and promotion. Membership includes authors and illustrators, publishers and editors, translators, journalists and critics, teachers, university professors and students, librarians and booksellers, social workers and parents. IBBY administers the Hans Christian Andersen and the Asahi Reading Promotion Awards, publishes the biennial IBBY Honour List of outstanding recently published children's books and a quarterly journal *Bookbird*, as well as leading International Children's Book Day.

Making partnerships work

Partnerships need to be managed if they are to work effectively. This requires excellent communication, clear project planning and a willingness to adapt while retaining a clear sense of one's own priorities. Successful management of partnerships requires:

- identification of relevant and proven partners
- definition of common ground, exploration of realistic mutual benefits and definition of the purpose of the partnership
- effective communication
- evaluation and monitoring of the partnership, with formal structures for feedback to all partners
- refreshing and rebuilding as people within the partnerships move on and new ones take their place
- time – partnerships aren't built overnight, they require an investment of time, effort and energy.

As well as being an essential aspect of the school librarian's life, partnerships can be enjoyable, broadening partners' experience and providing allies who can help them to achieve their objectives.

References

AQA (2013) *The AQA Extended Project Qualification*,
www.aqa.org.uk/programmes/aqa-baccalaureate/extended-project/
the-aqa-epq [accessed 16 May 2013].

Barrett, L. and Douglas, J. (2004) *The CILIP Guidelines for Secondary School Libraries*, 2nd edn, Facet Publishing.

Bartlett, J. and Miller, C. (2011) *Truth, Lies and the Internet: a report into young people's digital fluency*,
www.demos.co.uk/files/Truth_-_web.pdf [accessed 13 May 2013].

Bloom, B. (ed.) (1956) *Taxonomy of Educational Objectives: the classification of educational goals: Handbook I, cognitive domain*, Longmans, Green.

British Dyslexia Association (n.d.) *Dyslexia Style Guide*,
www.bdadyslexia.org.uk/about-dyslexia/further-information/dyslexia-style-guide.html [accessed 14 September 2013].

CBI (2013) *Business Fears Skills Shortage Could Hold Back Growth*,
www.cbi.org.uk/media-centre/press-releases/2013/06/businesses-fear-skills-shortage-could-hold-back-growth [accessed 17 February 2014].

Chartered Institute of Marketing (2000) *Marketing and the 7 Ps: a brief summary of marketing and how it works*,
www.cim.co.uk/files/7ps.pdf [accessed 1 October 2013].

CILIP (2011) *School Libraries: a right*,
www.cilip.org.uk/sites/default/files/documents/school-libraries-a-right.pdf [accessed 18 August 2013].

CILIP (2012) *Carnegie and Kate Greenaway Children's Book Awards*, www.carnegiegreenaway.org.uk/home/index.php [accessed 17 September 2013].

CILIP (2013a) *Certification*, www.cilip.org.uk/cilip/jobs-and-careers/ qualifications-and-professional-development/certification [accessed 17 September 2013].

CILIP (2013b) *Information Literacy: definition*, www.CILIP.org.uk/cilip/advocacy-awards-and-projects/advocacy-and-campaigns/information-literacy [accessed 10 March 2014].

CILIP (2013c) *Professional Knowledge and Skills Base*, www.cilip.org.uk/cilip/jobs-and-careers/professional-knowledge-and-skills-base [accessed 14 September 2013].

Clark, C. (2012) *Children's and Young People's Reading Today: findings from the 2011 National Literacy Trust's annual survey*, National Literacy Trust.

Claxton, G. (2000) *Building Learning Power: helping young people become better learners*, TLO Ltd.

Costa, A. L. (2000) *Habits of Mind* series (5 vols), Association for Supervision and Curriculum Development.

Department for Education (2012) *Encouraging Reading for Pleasure*, www.education.gov.uk/schools/teachingandlearning/pedagogy/ b00192950/encouraging-reading-for-pleasure [accessed 26 July 2013].

Department for Education and Skills (2004) *Building Bulletin 98: briefing framework for secondary school projects*, http://media.education.gov.uk/assets/files/pdf/b/building%20bulletin%20 98%20-%20briefing%20framework%20for%20secondary%20school %20projects.pdf [accessed 16 May 2013].

Edexcel (2013) *Project Qualification – Level 3*, www.edexcel.com/quals/project/level3/Pages/default.aspx [accessed 16 May 2013].

Education Scotland (2013) *Information and Critical Literacy*, www.educationscotland.gov.uk/informationliteracy/index.asp [accessed 5 June 2013].

Eisenberg, M. and Berkovitz, R. (1990) *Information Problem Solving: the Big Six approach to library and information skills instruction*, Norwood, NJ, Ablex.

Engelbrecht, K. (2003) *The Impact of Color on Learning*, http://sdpl.coe.uga.edu/HTML/W305.pdf [accessed 14 September 2013].

Gardner, H. (1985) *Frames of Mind*, New York, Basic Books.

Goleman, D. (1996) *Emotional Intelligence: why it can matter more than IQ,* Bloomsbury.

Goleman, D. (1999) *Working with Emotional Intelligence,* Bloomsbury.

Greenfield, S. (2000) *The Human Brain: a guided tour,* Phoenix Press.

Health and Safety Executive (n.d.) *Temperature,* www.hse.gov.uk/temperature/index.htm [accessed 24 July 2013].

Herring, J. E. (1999) *Exploiting the Internet as an Information Resource in Schools,* Library Association Publishing.

Hicks, B. (2013) *Paperless Public Libraries Switch to Digital,* BBC News, 22 May 2013, www.bbc.co.uk/news/business-22160990 [accessed 1 September 2013].

IFLA (2005) *Alexandria Proclamation,* www.ifla.org/publications/beacons-of-the-information-society-the-alexandria-proclamation-on-information-literacy [accessed 26 April 2013].

IFLA (2013) *Information Literacy Section,* www.ifla.org/information-literacy [accessed 30 September 2013].

IFLA/UNESCO (2000) *The School Library Manifesto,* www.ifla.org/VII/s11/pubs/manifest.htm [accessed 15 September 2013].

Institute of Education (2013) *Reading for Pleasure Puts Children Ahead in the Classroom,* Study Finds, www.ioe.ac.uk/newsEvents/89938.html [accessed 14 September 2013].

International Baccalaureate (2005) *IB Diploma Programme Curriculum, Extended Essay,* www.ibo.org/diploma/curriculum/core/essay [accessed 17 May 2013].

Irving, C. and Crawford, J. (2007) *Skills for Everyone,* www.educationscotland.gov.uk/Images/information_literacy_framework_draft_tcm4-433724.pdf [accessed 4 October 2013].

JCS (2013) *JCS Online Resources,* http://jcsonlineresources.org [accessed 30 September 2013].

Kharbach, M. (2012) *The Modern Taxonomy Wheel,* www.schrockguide.net/bloomin-apps.html [accessed 15 May 2013].

Lance, K. C. and Hofschire, L. (2012) *Change in School Librarian Staffing Linked with Change in CSAP Reading Performance, 2005 to 2011,* www.lrs.org/documents/closer_look/CO4_2012_Closer_Look_Report.pdf [accessed 6 September 2013].

Lankes, R. D. (2011) *The Atlas of New Librarianship,* MIT.

Library Research Service (2013) *School Libraries and Student Achievement,* www.lrs.org/data-tools/school-libraries/impact-studies [accessed 6 September 2013].

LISC (Library and Information Services Council) (1984) *School Libraries: the foundations of the curriculum*, HMSO.

Loerstscher, D. V., Koechlin, C. and Zwaan, S. (2011) *The New Learning Commons: where learners win!*, 2nd edn, Learning Commons Press.

MLA (Museums, Libraries and Archives Council) (2008) *Inspiring Learning*, www.inspiringlearningforall.gov.uk [accessed 16 August 2013].

National Literacy Trust (2010) *School Libraries: a plan for improvement*, www.literacytrust.org.uk/assets/0000/5718/School_Libraries_A_Plan_for _Improvement.pdf [accessed 6 October 2013].

National Union of Teachers (c.2010) *Reading for Pleasure*, www.teachers.org.uk/files/active/1/Reading-4-Pleasure-7225.pdf [accessed 26 July 2013].

Ofsted (2012) *Moving English Forward*, www.ofsted.gov.uk/resources/moving-english-forward [accessed 15 September 2013].

Ofsted (2013a) *Framework for School Inspection*, www.ofsted.gov.uk/resources/framework-for-school-inspection [accessed 22 September 2013].

Ofsted (2013b) *Improving Literacy in Secondary Schools: a shared responsibility*, www.ofsted.gov.uk/resources/improving-literacy-secondary-schools-shared-responsibility [accessed 1 September 2013].

Prashnig, B. (1998) *The Power of Diversity*, David Bateman Ltd.

Robinson, K. (2011) *Out of Our Minds: learning to be creative*, 2nd edn, Capstone.

School Libraries Group (2013) *Professional Librarians Leaflet*, www.cilip.org.uk/school-libraries-group/professional-librarians-leaflet [accessed 20 October 2013].

School Library Association (2008) *Pupil Librarian Toolkit*, www.sla.org.uk/pupil-librarian-toolkit-member-benefit.php [accessed 15 September 2013].

School Library Association (2013) *EPQ Course*, www.sla.org.uk/cpd-epq. php [accessed 17 May 2013].

Scottish Library and Information Council (2009) *Improving Libraries for Learners*, www.slainte.org.uk/files/pdf/slic/schoollibs/ ImprovingLibsForLearners.pdf [accessed 16 August 2013].

Shaper, S. and Streatfield, D. (2012) Invisible Care? The role of librarians in caring for the 'whole pupil' in secondary schools, *Pastoral Care in Education*, **30** (1), 65–75.

Shrock, K. (2011) *Bloomin' Apps*, www.schrockguide.net/bloomin-apps.html [accessed 15 May 2013].

The Stationery Office (2010) *Equality Act 2010*, www.legislation.gov.uk/ukpga/2010/15/pdfs/ukpga_20100015_en.pdf [accessed 14 September 2013].

Streatfield, D. and Markless, S. (2004) *Improve Your Library: a self-evaluation process for secondary school libraries and learning resource centres*, 2 vols, Department for Education and Skills.

Streatfield, D. R. and Rae-Scott, S. (2013) Going the Extra Mile: what makes school librarians proactive?, *School Libraries Worldwide*, forthcoming.

Streatfield, D. R., Shaper, S. and Rae-Scott, S. (2010) *School Libraries in the UK: a worthwhile past, a difficult present – and a transformed future?* www.cilip.org.uk/sites/default/files/documents/full-school-libraries-report_0.pdf [accessed 24 July 2013].

Taylor, M. (2011) *Reading at 16 Linked to Better Job Prospects*, www.ox.ac.uk/media/news_stories/2011/110804.html [accessed 1 September 2013].

Tilke, A. (1998) *Library Association Guidelines for Secondary School Libraries*, Library Association Publishing.

Webber, S. (2010) *Information Literacy for the 21st Century* (presentation), www.academia.edu/1003857/Information_literacy_for_the_21st_century [accessed 26 April 2013].

Welsh Libraries (2009) *Welsh Information Literacy Project*, http://welshlibraries.org.en/skills/information-literacy [accessed 17 March 2014].

Williams, D., Wavell, C. and Coles, L. (2001) *Impact of School Library Services on Achievement and Learning: critical literature review*, The Robert Gordon University, www4.rgu.ac.uk/files/Impact%20of%20School%20Library%20Services1.pdf [accessed 1 September 2013].

Wray, D. and Lewis, M. (1995) Extending Interactions with Non-fiction Texts: an exit to understanding, *Reading*, **29** (1), 2–9.

Example job description and person specification for a school librarian

The School Librarian is responsible for the leadership, management and operation of the major learning environment used by the whole school community. The School Librarian is responsible for ensuring that the school library impacts positively on teaching and learning across all areas of the curriculum and that the school library provides for the learning needs, both educational and recreational, of the full age and ability range within that community. In order to do this, the School Librarian is responsible for the acquisition, organization, dissemination and exploitation of the resources and facilities (real and virtual) in efficient and cost-effective ways.

Post title: School Librarian
Status: Head of Department
Responsible to: Deputy Head Teacher with responsibility for the curriculum
Responsible for: library assistants, student library assistants, work placement trainees, students studying library and information services, volunteers
Internal contacts: all school staff and students
External contacts: School Library Service [if there is one in the area], local feeder schools and FE institutions, colleagues in local and regional secondary schools, publishers, public libraries, suppliers and professional organizations
Prime objectives:
- to provide the leadership, expertise and professionalism necessary to ensure that the school library supports and enhances the key goals and objectives of the whole school

- to provide the leadership, expertise and professionalism necessary to ensure that the school library is an integral component of the school's learning and teaching priorities
- to promote and develop critical thinking and effective research/study skills for all students so that they can become proficient and ethical users of information
- to instil a love of reading and learning in all students, thereby developing their potential as lifelong and independent learners
- to ensure equitable access to information, both physical and virtual, for the whole school community
- to create a whole-school environment that encourages reading for pleasure.

Main functions: the School Librarian will:

1   Liaise with and advise senior management and other colleagues on policies for the provision of learning resources across the curriculum which support and enhance the key educational aims and objectives of the school.
2   Evaluate and monitor the effectiveness of the library's contribution to teaching and learning.
3   Negotiate and manage the library budget, ensuring that it provides good value for money and cost-effectiveness.
4   Support the school's pastoral and personalized learning policies by providing resources in a range of formats which enable students to learn more about their personal needs and concerns in a secure environment.
5   Mediate between learners and resources to enable learners to identify, locate and access the information they need.
6   Promote the development of reading and literacy skills for information and recreation and take a lead in creating a whole-school environment that encourages reading for pleasure.
7   Lead the teaching of transferable information, learning and knowledge access skills, which are the core skills of independent lifelong learning.
8   Manage and promote a wide range of resources in a variety of formats, traditional and electronic, and where appropriate, the equipment to access them.

9 Manage a study environment for both curriculum-based and independent learning. This involves the management and integration of both physical areas and virtual learning environments to create positive learning spaces.

10 Enable teaching staff to maintain a high level of awareness of professional development and relevant resources through the provision of appropriate professional materials and information.

11 Participate in school-wide improvement through attending the regular cycle of meetings with senior staff.

12 Collaborate with feeder primary schools to support transition between primary and secondary school.

13 Work with FE institutions to support transition and the development of appropriate transferable information literacy skills.

14 Create and implement a school library policy that includes compliance with data protection, copyright and health and safety legislation in line with the whole-school policies.

15 Analyse educational initiatives and trends in library and information services so that the school library is based on the most up-to-date information and methods.

16 Maximize use of local and national support networks, including School Library Services [if available], online forums, professional organizations and publishers.

17 Support the engagement of parents/carers in their children's learning and curriculum needs and involve the school library, as appropriate, in home–school liaison projects.

Person specification – School Librarian

Qualifications:

- Chartered Member of the Chartered Institute of Library and Information Professionals (CILIP)
- professional qualification in librarianship, information management or information science

Experience: minimum of two years working in an education library

Basic skills and competencies: prospective candidates need to demonstrate experience and understanding of the following areas:

- secondary education, with an awareness of current issues and trends
- reading interests of secondary students, covering the full range of ages and abilities, and the national and regional initiatives which support the reading interests of secondary age students
- IT competence, including a good working knowledge of e-resources, e-books, digital technologies, Web 2.0, virtual learning environments and other educational online services and facilities
- information literacy teaching
- advocacy and PR strategies
- improvement planning, monitoring and evaluation strategies
- budget management
- library management systems
- resource selection in all formats
- behaviour management
- health and safety issues
- time management skills.

Personal qualities: prospective candidates need to demonstrate:

- an enthusiasm for and an understanding of the complexities of working with teenagers
- excellent communication and interpersonal skills
- an aptitude for team working and the ability to take the initiative as a creative thinker
- an enthusiastic, self-motivated and flexible approach to work and the working environment
- experience of project management
- good administrative, organizational and planning skills.

[Employers would need to add their standard statements regarding equal opportunities and the candidate's availability to work the required hours.]

Example job description and person specification for an assistant school librarian

The Assistant School Librarian deputizes for the School Librarian in the day-to-day management of the school library. The Assistant School Librarian is responsible for ensuring that appropriate print and online resources are available at all times to support the teaching and learning within the school and that the whole school community has access to these resources. The Assistant School Librarian, in conjunction with the School Librarian, is responsible for the acquisition, organization, dissemination and exploitation of the resources and facilities (real and virtual) in efficient and cost-effective ways.

Post title: Assistant School Librarian
Responsible to: School Librarian
Responsible for: library assistants, student library assistants, work placement trainees/students studying library and information services, volunteers
Internal contacts: all school staff and students
External contacts: School Library Service (SLS) [if there is one in the area], local feeder schools and FE institutions, colleagues in local and regional secondary schools, publishers, public libraries, suppliers and professional organizations
Prime objectives:
- to ensure that the school library supports and enhances the key goals and objectives of the whole school as defined by the school's senior management
- to ensure that the school library is an integral component of the school's learning and teaching priorities

- to support the promotion and development of critical thinking and effective research/study skills for all students so that they can become ethical users of information
- to support initiatives which instil a love of reading and learning in all students, thereby developing their potential as lifelong and independent learners
- to ensure equitable access to information, both physical and virtual, for the whole school community
- to implement and support initiatives which create a whole-school environment that encourages reading for pleasure.

Main functions: the Assistant School Librarian will:

1 Deputize for the School Librarian in the day-to-day management of the school library.
2 Liaise with the School Librarian on policies and planning for the provision of learning resources across the curriculum that support and enhance the key educational aims and objectives of the school.
3 Support the School Librarian in the evaluation and monitoring of the effectiveness of the library's contribution to teaching and learning.
4 Manage, in conjunction with the School Librarian, the library budget, ensuring that it provides good value for money and cost-effectiveness.
5 Support, in conjunction with the School Librarian, the school's pastoral and personalized learning policies by providing resources in a range of formats that enable students to learn more about their personal needs and concerns in a secure environment.
6 Help students and staff to identify, locate and access the information they need.
7 In conjunction with the School Librarian and curriculum departments, plan and deliver information and learning skills lessons that teach the core skills of independent lifelong learning.
8 Manage and promote a wide range of resources in a variety of formats, traditional and electronic, and where appropriate, the equipment to access them.
9 Catalogue and process new stock in conjunction with all school library staff.

10 In conjunction with the School Librarian, develop and maintain an online presence for the school library, promoting its resources and services to staff and students.

11 Assist in the provision of appropriate professional materials and information for teaching and support staff in the school.

12 Participate, as required, in school-wide improvement through deputizing at the regular cycle of meetings with senior staff.

13 In conjunction with the School Librarian, train and manage student library assistants.

14 Plan and implement, in conjunction with the School Librarian, initiatives with feeder primary schools to support transition between primary and secondary school.

15 Plan and implement, in conjunction with the School Librarian, initiatives with FE institutions to support transition and the development of appropriate transferable information literacy skills.

16 Implement the school library policy, which includes compliance with data protection, copyright and health and safety legislation in line with the whole-school policies.

17 Keep up to date with educational initiatives and trends in library and information services so that the school library is based on the most up-to-date information and methods.

18 Participate in local and national library networks, including School Library Services [if available], online forums, professional organizations, publishers.

19 Implement initiatives aimed at engaging parents/carers in their children's learning and curriculum needs and involve the school library, as appropriate, in home–school liaison projects.

Person specification – Assistant School Librarian

Qualifications: professional qualification in librarianship, information management or information science

OR

Experience: minimum of two years' experience working in a library and evidence of working toward a professional qualification.

Basic skills and competencies: prospective candidates need to demonstrate experience and understanding of the following areas:

- secondary education, with an awareness of current issues and trends
- reading interests of secondary students, covering the full range of ages and abilities, and the national and regional initiatives which support the reading interests of secondary age students
- IT competence and a willingness to develop a good working knowledge of e-resources, e-books, digital technologies, Web 2.0, virtual learning environments and other educational online services and facilities
- information literacy teaching
- advocacy and PR strategies
- development planning, monitoring and evaluation strategies
- budget management
- library management systems
- resource selection in all formats
- behaviour management
- health and safety issues
- time management skills.

Personal qualities: prospective candidates need to demonstrate:

- an enthusiasm for and an understanding of the complexities of working with teenagers
- excellent communication and interpersonal skills
- an aptitude for team working and the ability to take the initiative as a creative thinker
- an enthusiastic, self-motivated and flexible approach to work and the working environment
- good administrative, organizational and planning skills.

[Employers would need to add their standard statements regarding equal opportunities and the candidate's availability to work the required hours.]

Example job description and person specification for a school library assistant

The School Library Assistant assists in the day-to-day running of the school library and is committed to providing a service which meets the needs of the whole school community. The School Library Assistant is aware of the school's key priorities. The School Library Assistant supports the work of the School Librarian, who is responsible for ensuring that the school library impacts positively on the teaching and learning across all areas of the curriculum and that the school library provides for the learning needs, both educational and recreational, of the full age and ability range within that community.

Post title: School Library Assistant
Responsible to: School Librarian
Responsible for: student library assistants
Internal contacts: all school staff and students
Main functions: the School Library Assistant will:

1   Take responsibility for the efficient operation of the library counter, including issuing resources, answering enquiries from students and staff.
2   Implement all regular procedures, ensuring that the school library is maintained in good order.
3   Check the school library's IT facilities on a daily basis and report any faults or problems to the relevant department.
4   Shelve and tidy stock.
5   Maintain library signage in good order, including shelf labels, book ends, posters and displays.
6   Process new resources.

7   Maintain the overdue system.
8   Help library users find the resources to meet their needs and support them through a range of library-based activities.
9   Support, in conjunction with the School Librarian, reader development initiatives and those involving feeder schools and FE institutions.
10 Supervise the work of the Student Library Assistants.
11 Support and assist with other tasks as may be required by the School Librarian.

Person specification – School Library Assistant

Qualifications: 5+ GCSE A*-C (or equivalent), including English and Maths
Experience: previous work in a school, college or education library would be an advantage
Basic skills and competencies: prospective candidates need to demonstrate:

- good IT skills or a willingness to learn
- good numeracy and literacy skills
- an interest in reading
- excellent communication and interpersonal skills.

Personal qualities: prospective candidates need to demonstrate:

- an enthusiasm for working with teenagers
- excellent communication and interpersonal skills
- an aptitude for team working
- an enthusiastic, self-motivated and flexible approach to work and the working environment
- good administrative, organizational and planning skills
- a willingness to learn new skills
- a cheerful and welcoming disposition and a helpful, 'can-do' attitude.

[Employers would need to add their standard statements regarding equal opportunities and the candidate's availability to work the required hours.]

Model questions and answers for recruitment interviews

For a librarian

How would you ensure that the library is well used by all curriculum areas?	*Look for enthusiasm, realistic view of pressures within a school, good interpersonal skills*
What reading books would you recommend to a Year 8 boy who does not enjoy reading?	*Look for up-to-date book knowledge and experience of working with young people*
How would you go about implementing some changes that you think are not going to be popular?	*Look for an awareness of the problems of managing change and good people skills*
Which skills do you think students need to learn to make best use of the school library?	*Look for a knowledge of information literacy skills and good practice in delivering them*
What would you include in a programme of activities for a Year 7–9 book club that meets for 50 minutes each week?	*Look for evidence of creativity, e.g. using web tools, multimedia, fun activities, knowledge of book awards, etc., plus experience of what young people enjoy*
What would you include in your lesson plan if you were asked to deliver two sessions to Year 10 Geography students who are lacking in research skills?	*Look for knowledge of information literacy, experience of delivery and people skills necessary to successfully collaborate with teaching colleagues*
What do you think of the following statement: 'Graphic novels are too easy for children and have no place in a school library'?	*Look for the vision of reading promotion. Is it compatible with the school's vision?*

For a library assistant

A pupil in the library tells you that they hate reading . . . how might you begin to encourage this pupil to change his attitude towards reading?	*Look for an interest in young people, a friendly attitude towards them and an eagerness to share a love of reading*
What would you do if the other library staff had gone out of the room for a few minutes and two Year 9 students started shouting at one another?	*Look for a confident and calm approach, sensible ways of getting help if the situation escalates and questions about standard school sanctions and procedures. Should not include shouting. Should not be timid or scared at the prospect*

Continued on next page

124 CILIP GUIDELINES FOR SECONDARY SCHOOL LIBRARIES

Some of the work is routine. How do you cope with periods of repetitive work?	*Look for a realistic approach to the role*
Tell us about your favourite book.	*Look for a passion for reading and an articulate way of sharing this*
What skills or attributes are needed when working with teenagers?	*Look for empathy with teenagers and self-awareness regarding strengths*
The world of libraries is constantly changing and we need to be able to keep up with the times. Can you tell me about a new skill you have mastered?	*Look for a willingness and ability to learn new skills and adapt to changes*

Example school library staff progression framework and case studies

*Revised and expanded version of work done by
Sally McIntosh for use in the East Midlands*

School library staff progression framework

Job title	Main job roles	Qualification framework	Equivalence	Suggested pay scales
Library Auxiliary	Keeping the library and resources tidy, photocopying, helping to maintain discipline, cleaning and tidying.	Literacy and Numeracy Key Skills Level 1	Lunchtime Supervisor	Local Government Pay Scale Pts 4–6
Library Assistant	Issuing/returning/ renewing resources. Preparing resources (labelling/ covering, etc.). Keeping resources organized. Helping students and staff locate resources. Creating and maintaining displays.	Apprenticeship or NVQ 2 Library and Information Skills or Administration Literacy/Numeracy Key Skills Level 2	Admin Assistant	Local Government Pay Scale Pts 12–14
Library Technician	As Library Assistant + Maintenance of computer hardware and audio-visual equipment. Helping students and staff with ICT and audiovisual equipment.	Apprenticeship or NVQ 2 Library and Information Skills or ICT Skills Literacy/Numeracy Key Skills Level 2	ICT Technician	Local Government Pay Scale Pts 12–15
Senior Library Assistant	As Library Assistant + Supervision of library assistant or auxiliary. Data entry into catalogue. Preparation of worksheets and other materials for learning (directed by librarian or teacher). Supporting individual students using the library.	Apprenticeship or NVQ 2 Library and Information Skills + significant experience 5+ GCSE A*–C (or equivalent) including English and Maths	Level 2 Teaching Assistant	Local Government Pay Scale Pts 14–17

Continued on next page

Job title	Main job roles	Qualification framework	Equivalence	Suggested pay scales
Library Manager (recommended minimum level for day-to-day management of a school library)	Day-to-day management of library space and resources. Management of library assistant/ auxiliary/technician. Purchase of resources as agreed with teachers or librarians. Cataloguing and organization of resources. Maintaining discipline. Helping students and staff locate resources within the library. Supporting individual students and groups using the library.	NVQ 3 Library Information Skills + Level 3 Academic Education (equivalent to 2 A-Levels)

GCSE English A*-B + Maths A*-C | Higher Level Teaching Assistant | Local Government Pay Scale Pts 20–25 |
| Librarian | Organization and management of the library space, resources and staff. Selecting and purchasing resources. Advising teaching staff on suitable resources. Classifying and cataloguing resources. Working in partnership with teaching staff on the development of lessons and activities relating to literacy and research skills. Developing positive relationships with students and staff. Encouraging reading for pleasure. Helping classes, individuals and groups using the library to develop literacy, research and ICT skills. | Information and Library Studies Degree

OR

Other Level 4 Qualification + Postgraduate Diploma or Masters in Information and Library Studies | Teacher (Main Scale) | Local Government Pay Scale Pts 26–31 |
| Technical Librarian | As Librarian + Providing specialist advice to senior management on ICT development policy. Responsibility for development and/or maintenance of whole-school website, learning platform or software evaluation and selection. Providing training for teaching staff in ICT-related areas, e.g. website evaluation, computer skills, software use. | As Librarian + Level 3 or higher Qualification in ICT-related area or significant relevant experience.

CILIP Chartership | Teacher (Upper Scale) | Local Government Pay Scale Pts 32–36 |

Continued on next page

Job title	Main job roles	Qualification framework	Equivalence	Suggested pay scales
Curriculum Librarian	As Librarian + Providing specialist advice to senior management on literacy, research or thinking skills policy. Developing schemes of work for use across departments or year groups relating to literacy, research or thinking skills. Advising and training teaching staff in related areas.	Level 4 Qualification + Postgraduate Diploma or Masters in Information and Library Studies CILIP Chartership	Teacher (Upper Scale)	Local Government Pay Scale Pts 32–36
Development Librarian	As Librarian + Responsibility for school wide development of literacy, research skills, thinking skills or cross-curricular ICT. Working in partnership with senior management on the development of related school wide policies. Providing systematic training for teaching staff in the related area. [Creating and maintaining links between local consortia schools, external agencies or community groups.]	Level 4 Qualification in Information and Library Studies + PGCE/MEd/PhD in an Education Subject OR Level 4 Qualification in Education, Teaching Studies or subject related to the area of development + PGDip./MSc/ MA /PhD in Information and Library Studies CILIP Chartership/ Fellowship	Head of Department/ Assistant Head	Local Government Pay Scale Pts 37 + Dependent upon skills, experience and level of responsibility

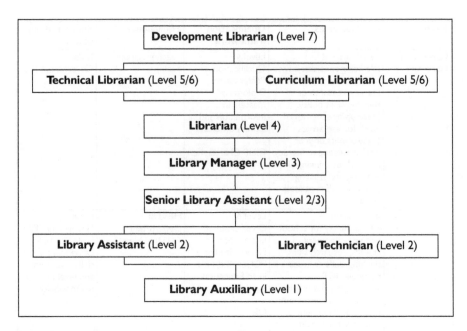

Staffing structure case studies

Secondary school with 1500+ students and a split-site library	Secondary school with 800 students	Middle school with 450 students	Primary school consortium (4 primary schools, with rolls from 70 to 250)
Leading the library	**Leading the library**	**Leading the library**	**Leading the libraries**
Development Librarian responsible for thinking skills development with a Teaching Studies Degree, an MSc in Information and Library Studies and a CILIP Chartership	Curriculum Librarian working on literacy development with a degree in English, a Postgraduate Diploma in Information and Library Studies and a CILIP Chartership	Library Manager with NVQ 3 in Information and Library Skills and 3 A-Levels	Librarian (shared between the 4 schools) with a degree in Information and Library Studies (42 weeks per year)
Assisting	**Assisting**	**Assisting**	**Assisting**
Library Manager with a degree and NVQ 3 in Information and Library Skills Library Technician with Apprenticeship in ICT Part time Library Auxiliary employed for 10 hours per week	Senior Library Assistant with NVQ 2 Library Assistant's Certificate and 15 years' experience (20 hours per week – term time only)	Part-time Library Auxiliary (10 hours per week – term time only) with Key Skills Level 2 in Literacy and Level 1 in Numeracy	Each of the 3 smaller schools employs a lunchtime supervisor as a library auxiliary for 3–5 hours a week, term-time only. The largest school employs an admin assistant, who spends around 12 hours a week in the library and is working towards the NVQ 2 Library Assistant's Certificate

Example budget for setting up a new secondary school library

Table of costs – initial setup for secondary schools

	Approximate cost
Library management system (LMS) set-up	£4500
Security system (gates and book triggers)	£4–10,000 (if required)
Shelving, seating, tables and chairs	£15–30,000, depending on size of library
eBook hosting and set-up fees	£3000
ICT, e.g. netbooks, e-readers or terminals	Variable
Initial spend on resources	£30,000 per year for 3 years
Photocopier, projector, screen, printer(s)	Variable
Subscriptions, e.g. school library service	Variable
Promotions, e.g. author visits	Approx. £500 per event

Table of costs – approximate yearly running for secondary schools

	Approximate cost
Library management system helpdesk fee	£500–900
Annual budget after set-up period based on school of 800 students	£12,000
Running costs, e.g. stationery, book covers, barcodes	£1000
Subscriptions, e.g. School Lbrary Service	Variable
Promotions, e.g. author visits	Approx. £500 per event

Notes:
- Figures correct at 2013, so current prices should be checked
- Costing assumes that continuing professional development is paid for centrally.

Example school library improvement plan 2013–14

Whole-school objective point: improving learning (curriculum)

Team: Library

Target and action steps	Monitoring and success criteria	Staff involved	Completion date	Resource, training and development needs	Costs
Refine and develop learning skills lessons for Year 7	Evaluate strengths and weaknesses of previous lessons and agree amendments. New materials produced for 2013/14.	Librarian/Assistant Librarian/Head of Humanities	Jun 2013 Sept 2013	2 hrs meeting time Photocopying of resources Information pack for staff involved in delivery	
Improve reading challenge	Amend reading challenge and pass to English staff for approval. Reading challenge: Bronze achieved by 90% of Y9 students. Silver by 50%, Gold by 10%.	Librarian/English staff	Jul 2013 Jul 2014	1 hr meeting time Development time	
Develop Sixth Form research skills	Plagiarism and research booklets issued. Research skill needs of Sixth Form evaluated. Plan developed with Head of Sixth Form for targeted research skills input.	Librarian/Head of Sixth Form. Librarian/Sixth Form teaching staff. Librarian/Head of Sixth Form	Sept 2013 Dec 2013 Jun 2014	Booklets (already available) Survey development time and photocopying Meeting time	
Improve signs in library to aid independent retrieval of resources	Ideas sought from students about useful labelling/signs. New signs created and installed.	Assistant Librarian	Nov 2013 Jan 2014	Meeting time with students Agenda item for students council Development time Access to colour printer and laminator	

Library policy template

School name		
Date of policy (or latest revision)		

I The aims of the school library
Include here statements about the overall vision and what the service is setting out to achieve. Ensure that these aims link closely to the school's overall aims and vision. Ensure, too, that there is a key statement about who the library aims to serve.

2 The key objectives for the school library
These could be medium-term aims or the main areas of service and focus for the school library (e.g. supporting the curriculum, providing for the wider curriculum, supporting individual students' skills, liaising with and working through teaching colleagues).
    They need to be developmental (e.g. to improve or increase rather than just to maintain), and measurable. They are the performance criteria against which progress will be measured.

3 School library management and communication
Include here:

- *the management and staffing of the school library*
- *networks and processes for consultation with users (staff and students)*
- *links to other school committees and services*
- *links to other school policies and the development plan.*

4 Access issues
Include here details about day-to-day access for students and teachers (opening hours, etc.). Specify the access for class groups. Also, outline the agreed induction programmes that are in place for the various year groups. Identify how the library is staffed at different times – what can students and staff expect? Outline the basic principles for, and the details of, the signing and guiding.

5 Library use
This is the place to clarify any issues of policy regarding use of the library – the rules and regulations – but try to have only a few of these. Include a basic outline of use by staff. Identify any special conditions for using IT and other materials. Code of conduct/behaviour management.
    Identify any challenges and their solutions (e.g. equal access to IT for boys and girls; providing adequate support for students with special needs).
    Outline the basic issues of marketing as it affects the library:

- *consulting with users and identifying needs*
- *clarifying details of the services that will meet these needs*
- *promoting the services to potential users*
- *reviewing services by involving users.*

Clarify any special issues relating to specific school policies or aims (e.g. the link to students' independent learning; the whole school information skills curriculum).

Continued on next page

6 Resources, accommodation and finance

Identify standards relating to resource provision in the school – the stock, the accommodation, the space and the equipment that are needed at a basic level. If possible, include benchmarks provided by information from other schools or supplied by the SLS, or from national publications. Include an outline of an annual budget bid, showing how it is developed and the main elements that the budget needs to cover.

7 Support and partnerships

List any support agencies and contacts used (such as the SLS or local libraries and museums or education centres). Identify the membership of professional associations as appropriate.

8 Monitoring and evaluation

List any performance measures and performance indicators in use on a regular basis. Identify the ways in which the library seeks feedback from users (staff and students), and the ways in which the quality of the service is tested and measured. Keep a list of the key achievements over the past three years, and a list of the main developments towards which the library is aiming. The short-term and medium-term ones will feature in the library improvement plan, but the longer-term aims can at least be discussed when the policy is reviewed annually. Identify the ways in which the library policy will itself be reviewed on a regular basis.

Name

Signature

Post

Date of next review

Example procedures policies

Policy for overdue resources – School A

Aim: To encourage a responsible attitude to the use of the library as a resource for the whole school community to be achieved by:

1 Displaying the expectations of behaviour and applying them consistently.
2 Encouraging students to help with the running of the library.
3 Encouraging staff and students to make purchase suggestions.
4 Ensuring that all students are encouraged to take responsibility for returning borrowed items on time.

This is followed by a section in the Student User Code:

Library Student User Code
- Years 7–11 may borrow up to four items (books or DVDs) and the Sixth Form up to six.
- The standard loan period is 14 days, but some Sixth Form books are only issued as short loans: 1 hour in school, overnight, 3 days or 7 days.
- DVDs are issued for 3 days and the film classification is strictly adhered to.
- Anyone with overdue items will not be issued with further items until the outstanding ones have been renewed (if less than 7 days overdue) or returned. Sixth Form students with overdue short-term loans will not be issued with further books until the outstanding loans have been returned.
- Please return your book/s on or before the date stamped on the date due label. If you have not finished reading the book/s you may renew them online, bring them back and ask the librarian to renew them for you, or ask the librarian to renew books on your account. Standard issue books may

be renewed online three times. If a book has been reserved by another borrower, or is a short-term loan, you may not be able to renew it.

- When you return your books, make sure you place them in the returns slot in either library counter, or return them directly to the librarian. This will ensure that the books are removed from your borrower record.
- Reminders for overdue books will be sent through form tutors.
- Detentions will be issued for books more than 28 days overdue, followed by a letter to parents requesting the replacement cost if items are still outstanding a week later.

Policy for overdue resources – School B

Our main aim is not so much to recover overdue books but to keep our students borrowing books and reading; consequently we do not charge fines.

We do have quite an elaborate overdue system (see illustration), which involves direct e-mails to students with a link to renew the item(s); letters home with copies to College Admin areas; SMS messages sent direct to parents; the loss of the facility to e-mail their friends; and inability to borrow further until items are returned or paid for.

If students have lost the item(s) then they can pay the cost of replacement in instalments.

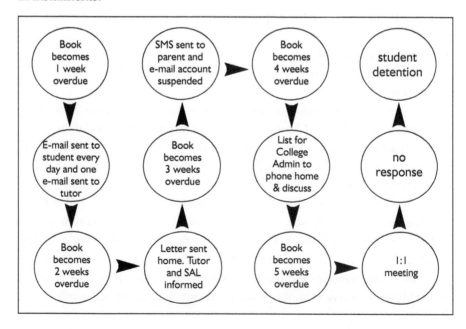

Facilities checklist

Area	In place	Planned/date	Comment
Shelving			

To meet requirements for accessibility:
• Maximum height 1500 mm (walls)
• Maximum height 1200 mm (island units)
• Sufficient space between bays to accommodate wheelchairs
• Fully adjustable shelving throughout the library
• Display shelves included (preferably one per bay)
• Shelf depth adequate for stock (min. 200 mm for fiction; 250 mm for non-fiction)
• Standard sized bays throughout, to allow for easy interchanging of shelves
• Clear sight lines
• Flexibility:
  — Ability to add units and equipment (display panels and flat walling)
  — Mobile units (castors)
• Shelving units to suit all resource types:
  — CDs, DVDs
  — Newspapers, magazines
  — Pamphlets, posters
  — Paperbacks, hardbacks			

Signing and guiding			
• Exterior notices and displays about the library • Map of library near entrance • Large hanging signs indicating different zones • Large bay headings to identify different stock areas • Clear shelf guides • Adjustable seats at computers, positioned to enable supervision • Some adjustable computer desks and tables, suitable for wheelchair users			
Equipment			
• Self-issue and dedicated enquiry terminals • Dedicated library staff terminals for the library management system • Sufficient workstations with school network and internet connections to accommodate at least one-half of a class at any one time • Photocopier			

Continued on next page

Area	In place	Planned/date	Comment
Equipment			
• Printers and scanners • Telephone and Wi-Fi • Multimedia projector, interactive whiteboard, etc.			
Security			
• Lockers/coat racks outside the library or just inside the entrance • Security mirrors • CCTV • Installation of electronic security system (proves to be cost-effective through loss reduction in most schools in 2–3 years, evidenced by annual stocktakes) • ICT hardware secured • Audiovisual equipment in locked storage when not in use			
Health and safety			
Fire			

• Exit routes uncluttered
• Sufficient fire extinguishers
  — Regularly tested
  — Staff trained in use
• Smoke alarms installed and tested
• Fire drill procedure notice on display
• Library inductions to include evacuation instructions			

Shelving			
• Secured into position • Not overloaded or top-heavy • Castors on mobile units always locked • No exposed edges on display shelves • Trolleys loaded evenly • All stock within easy reach			
Furniture			
• All of fire resistant/non-toxic material • Appropriate height or adjustable (users with disabilities catered for) • Trolleys designed for stability and used with care • Carpets and flooring securely fixed			
Technology and equipment			
• No trailing cables or exposed/damaged wiring • All electrical equipment checked annually			
Insurance			
• Library contents insured to replacement cost • Library staff insured appropriately for supervision of student numbers			

Index